JENNIFER R. LYONS

Cold Determination
Copyright © 2025 by Jennifer R. Lyons

Library of Congress Control Number: 2025900983

ISBN
978-1-964488-53-0 (Paperback)
978-1-964488-54-7 (eBook)
978-1-964488-52-3 (Hardcover)

Dedication

I would like to acknowledge my grandparents who this story is based on.

Table of Contents

/

The Beginning at the End

He couldn't bear the thought of leaving her behind. He knew he could never warm her again but he couldn't leave, not yet. His last gift was this bed—her final resting place.

Against the wishes of his son and daughter, he had wrapped her in a blanket inside her coffin. It was soft, covered in her favorite shade of pink. His daughter had advised against it. She told him it was too expensive and his son pointed out it was impractical. He had ignored them both. It was freezing out, and he couldn't bear the thought of lowering her into that unforgiving, hard ground without something warm to protect her. She was dressed in the same dress she wore on their wedding day. That had been June when it was warm and sunny. It was January now, sixty years later and too cold for such a dress, so he had insisted on the blanket.

The funeral was over and all the people were gone. He had stood vigilantly guarding her for four long hours, not knowing how to leave. The sky was darkening, and it was getting colder. His face and ears numb, he turned and finally walked away. He told himself he wasn't really leaving her—this was just a shell of her life. He reminded himself she was really safe and warm somewhere, surrounded with loved ones she had dearly missed. He imagined her with her favorite brother, sitting near a fire and talking about her life. No matter what he told himself, though, he couldn't stop himself fearing how cold that hole in the cold ground was. The wind was strengthening, and her body—the body he had loved and cared for all these years—was being left behind. That's all that mattered right now; she was gone from him and her body would stay cold.

He turned and left that hallowed ground of resting corpses, afraid for the first time in a long time. Old fears took over as he hastened his step. Stones, far older than him, called to him from a past long forgotten. A few steps over, a soldier—only twenty—waited for the day of second life. At his feet, a baby slept, having lived for just two days. He lengthened his stride; he didn't want to see these ghosts tonight.

As he walked, he felt he should feel lucky for all the life he lived. It had been a good life; one most would have been proud of. His poor immigrant parents had taught him to overcome hardships through their hard work and tenacity. Nothing had stopped them, not even the depression of the thirties. Instead, it had deepened a resolve in them to pass on resilient traits. He had grown knowing how to work, to be content, and to overcome. These traits had served him well.

Death had passed him by closely a few times, but he'd been allowed to live to see his children and even grandchildren grow.

I should feel lucky, he thought again. In this instance, though, he felt only the disquieting reality of loss, reminding him how quickly life passes. His body had grown old. Ninety years had taught him a lot, but he hadn't learned out to live without her. He didn't want life without her. It was unbearable and his heart ached.

For the first time during his long life, he felt old—he felt every one of his ninety years and hated this betrayal of his body. His hands shook, his back was bent, and his knees cried out in agony. Looking around, he realized he hated the betrayal of physical life. Nothing had saved this lot; nothing had saved his wife and nothing would save him. He tripped then, barely catching himself. He had seen something, causing him to lose his sure footing.

He was sure he'd seen a cat, winding her way through the old stones. With his stumble, he'd lost sight of her and when he looked again, he couldn't find her. He looked again, sure she'd be easy to spot amongst the dark stones with her white fur and bent tail. Try as he might, he couldn't find her.

Finally, he reached the car that had waited for him and he dropped into the seat, exhausted from loss and the frigid wind. Too tired to speak or even to think, he didn't acknowledge the driver nor the road. Leaning his head onto the seat, towards the window, he allowed sleep to overcome his normally vigilant mind.

Uninvited dreams entered his old mind. Unlike chaotic dreams of youth, these were sensible, full of light and meaning; they were easy to unravel. He recognized long lost family members, his childhood homes, and his war buddies. Locked between wake and sleep, his mind played back his life. As he watched, memories once grayed from time were colorfully restored.

Rosie

I was only four and had never really looked at a baby before. Somehow, I sensed how important and precious the tiny bundle in my mother's arms was. The bundle was quiet. The only sound in the room was Mama's tired breathing. Peter and I waited to enter the room until she beckoned us. I was so happy and relieved to see her, I ran to her bedside.

"Look, boys! Dziecko! Jesteś teraz wielkim bratem!" My mother's strong Polish accent with her soft mix of English made the moment so much more special. All night, our Mama had laid in this bed. I heard each frantic sound of our mother's labor without understanding what was happening. Now, she smiled at us—she was alright. Papa gently put me up on the bed so I could lay beside her. He always understood just what I needed.

Mama moved the bundle to her left, and I peered into a tiny, pink face. I had no idea what it was. I had never had a sister. She was wrapped head to toe in soft pieces of cloth. I couldn't see any arms or legs, just a head with closed eyes and pink cheeks. There was no hair on that ugly little head. There was nothing really extraordinary about this little bundle at all. I fell in love with the still, silent thing. My older brother, Peter, peered at the bed and claimed the baby was beautiful.

"I think this baby is ugly. I love it; can I hold it?"

My father laughed gently, and Mama hushed me as the bundle was sat on my lap, secured by Papa's strong arms. It hardly felt like anything at all, like I was holding a little cloud. Mama watched us proudly.

Peter asked, "What is her name?"

I looked at my mother, waiting to hear what we would call the bundle. "Her name is Rosie because she is pretty as a flower." I could tell my mother, who I thought looked like an angel, was very proud of this bundled potato. I didn't see any flowers. All I saw was a potato.

I told my mama, "I think she looks like a potato but I still love her." I kissed that ugly little head for the first time that day. Rosie, our potato-flower-bundle, stayed asleep.

For the first few days after she was born, our house was mostly normal. It was too cold to go outside, and Papa kept our little house warmer than usual. It felt good as we had no need for extra blankets as we played near our mother's bed on her floor. Peter and I were both good and quiet. No one told us, but somehow, we knew our new potato and Mama needed their rest. Every few minutes, one of us would run and peek into the top of the bed, seeing Mama and our potato baby sleeping.

As those first days stretched into weeks, then months, I realized that Rosie wasn't looking much like a potato anymore. After a couple of months, she could sit up when I helped her, and we would watch Peter do his funny dances for us. Rosie batted her small hands around, and I made sure she was safe. Her head had new hair that was curly and soft.

Rosie grew, turning into the happiest baby I have ever seen. She loved watching Peter perform his funny dances. When Papa came home from the coalmines, she would wave and gurgle a toothless smile at him. He would rush to hold her but Mama chased him away because he was too dirty. I never thought it strange that Mama let him chase Peter and I with dirty hands but never touch Rosie. After all, she was the baby, the pretty little flower we all watched over. She didn't need black smudges on her face, clothes, or blankets.

In time, Rosie demanded more food than only Mama's milk. Mama made her a thick porridge that Peter and I got to feed her in the evening while Mama fixed dinner. Rosie loved that porridge. She would howl impatiently, her toothless mouth wide open. After she finished the bowl, I carefully wiped off her pretty little face. I had to wipe off her hair a lot too. I didn't think Rosie knew she was a pretty little flower because she sure could make a mess when she ate. "Sometimes, Rosie, you are still like a potato—happy to be buried in dirt," I told her.

The whole year went by very fast and our little potato-bundle turned into a baby that crawled when we let her down. Mama was extra careful to keep the house clean. She made Peter and I look for small things Rosie might put in her mouth.

"We don't want her to choke," Mama would explain.

I was horrified at the thought of our baby Rosie choking on something. Every morning before breakfast, I patrolled the whole house, looking into each corner and ensuring the floor was void of all small objects. Peter looked too, and we were very proud to keep our baby safe.

As Rosie grew, the weather changed. First summer, then the days grew cold again and the nights long. We went to Mass on Sundays and knew it was Christmas season. Mama wanted our baby baptized before she turned a year old. I wasn't sure about that idea. Rosie seemed fine without getting sprinkled with water in a cold church.

I was happy to go to church, though. The town we lived in was actually a coal mining camp. It had a shop, a school, and houses but no proper church building. The church we were part of was a few miles away in a big town, and we rode a real trolley car to get there. I loved that car. It went on a track, loudly clanging a bell, and, even in the winter cold, it was fun to feel the air on my face. I never complained when Papa told us to get ready for church, thanks to that trolley car. Our family boarded the trolley early every Sunday morning and rode all the way into a town called Sheridan.

The Sunday Rosie was baptized, the priest taught about the first Christmas a long time ago. He talked about the baby Jesus born in a stable with only straw to lie on. Rosie was big now, but I still remembered our little potato baby. I felt bad any baby had a straw bed. I wondered if that baby Jesus had looked like a potato. I glanced at Peter, wondering if he thought I looked like a potato when he saw me for the first time.

After the priest told us about that baby Jesus, Mama and Papa brought Rosie to the front. It was hard to see what was going on, but we could hear.

Rosie didn't like being sprinkled. She also didn't like the strange priest holding her away from Mama. I whispered to Peter, "See? I told you this was a bad idea! She's going to holler now!" Peter just thumped my head lightly, shushing me.

I was right. Rosie didn't like the sprinkle, but I was wrong about the hollering. I guess Rosie knew we were supposed to be quiet in church, and I wondered if she had seen me get a thump. They finally finished and our family walked out into the cold, cold night. There was the bright moon and the sky full of stars; they seemed to be so close, I felt we could reach out to touch them. I was very excited to leave that church and ride the trolley again. It was cold, even for December.

When we got off the car, Mama fussed over everyone, pulling down our hats and pulling up our coat collars. As we neared our little home, wolves howled near enough that Mama hurried our short legs along. She was worried, I could tell. The baby's head even uncovered. Mama never let that happen; I think she was afraid of those wolves.

Once inside, Papa took Rosie from Mama and took a chair near the hot stove. Mama rushed around, readying our dinner. I could see bread and a thick mushroom soup. I had helped Mama with both. Mama showed me where mushrooms grew by the creek, and I filled her basket. When it was time to bake the bread, I had sprinkled flour as Mama kneaded the dough. Now, my tummy rumbled with anticipation.

Mama told us of Christmas in her old home, "Someday, moi mali synowie, I will make you the ciastko with the cukier sprinkled on top."

"You baptize the cookies, Mama?" I asked. Papa and Peter laughed, but no one answered my question. I didn't know what sugar was.

There were no gifts, and Peter and I wouldn't have known what to do with them anyways. Our Christmases were humble affairs full of love, but no presents and no tree. We had our dinner, much nicer than normal, and Mama would tell us stories from her childhood. She always started with the dinner.

It was an important, huge event; Mama was the youngest of nine kids and lived near all her relatives when she was little. Peter, my father, and I loved her stories. Our empty house soon filled with the smells and people from her past. I could hear my Papa whisper that he loved the gifts of her stories. She flushed rosy red at his compliment and paid it back with a kiss.

Our bellies filled with warm soup and soft bread. Papa settled us into our bed, and Rosie was settled in the middle of us. Papa said it was going to be too cold for her cradle and she needed us to keep her warm. We didn't mind—our potato had grown into a lovely soft angel, who reminded us of our mother. Rosie settled in quietly, her arm around Peter's right hand and her head resting on my shoulder.

"I won't let her be cold," I promised our father. He tucked us all in while Mama softly sang an old song in Polish, and, soon, we three were asleep.

Papa had been right to tuck Rosie in with us; the next day, he could hardly open the front door—there was so much snow! Peter and I dashed around, not waiting for breakfast, to venture into a world covered in soft ice. Mama yelled for us to bundle up as we squeezed through the small opening between door and frame. We were too excited to notice Rosie follow.

Peter and I ran to where our garden should have been and looked back. It seemed the snow was as tall as our house; at least eighteen inches fell throughout the night, and the wind caused huge drifts.

The boys from the next house over joined us, and we built forts and played war games well into the afternoon. Finally spent, we ran home on tired legs with frozen faces. Mama admonished us for bringing in the cold and wet. Then, she told us how she had rescued Rosie from the cold snow.

The little house smelled of our wet woolen coats. Mama tutted around, but we knew she wasn't that angry when she put on more firewood and heated water for us. She served us warmed sauerkraut, and all was right in our world.

We spent the next few days in the exact same manner. It was a lot of work on our bodies, playing so many hours in the snow each day. We would come in and tell Rosie all about our snow adventures, and Peter would dance his funny dances for her. We promised to take her with us when she got older. Soon after our dinner, the three of us were warm and fell sound asleep. Peter and I were so tired that nothing could wake us, and we never heard Rosie cough.

Rosie coughed all day the next morning, and Peter was angry with her. Mama would not allow the front door open with Rosie sick, denying us our freedom. Instead, we sat inside listening to our friends shout and laugh. It was terribly lonely, and Peter said he didn't feel like dancing. Rosie's cheeks were red and her nose runny. I helped Mama keep her face clean, but I could tell Rosie didn't like it. She would turn her head this way and that way more often, making more of a mess than getting clean. She coughed and coughed.

Peter and I were no longer so tired at night, and Rosie coughed all the time. We couldn't sleep and we sat up with Mama as she comforted Rosie. The next day, our Aunt Anya came to help. I never liked her. She was loud, bossy, and nothing like our own soft Mama even though they were sisters. Her hair was dark and there was a lot of it. Her eyes were big and slightly bulged. She hardly looked like an angel and she wasn't soft. Mama was always happy to see her and told Peter and I to be good. This time, she came with something for Rosie's cough, so I forgave her a little for being so loud.

Rosie cried and cried that day. Her cheeks grew redder and her eyes glassed over with fever. She slept, but we could all hear a rumble in her lungs. Mama was scared, I could tell, like she had been the night we heard the wolves. Her lips were tight, and she hardly put Rosie down at all. When Papa came home, the sauerkraut was still cold, but he didn't even complain; his lips were tight too.

Peter tried dancing that night for Rosie. He told her he was sorry he stopped and sorry he was mad at her for being sick. Rosie didn't see, and I didn't laugh. Nothing, not even Peter's dancing, was funny that night. Nothing was funny the next day either as Rosie mostly slept, oblivious to Mama holding her or Peter and I whispering over her head. Four more days passed that way, and Mama didn't even notice when Peter and I went out of doors.

Our house was so quiet, and even our Aunt Anya was quiet when she came over the next morning. She held our Mama as mama cried into her shoulder. Peter and I were afraid—there were no wolves, but we knew something bad was happening to our Rosie. I had a terrible pinching feeling deep in my stomach. She hadn't woken for four days and her breathing was so quiet, we had to hold our hands to her mouth to feel it. She even stopped the incessant coughing. I saw Aunt Anya wipe her eyes when Mama lay down next to Rosie.

And that was all. Rosie was bundled up and taken away the next day. She didn't look like a potato now. She looked like our Rosie, and I was frightened. Mama could hardly talk and even Papa had tears on his cheeks. Aunt Anya stayed and stayed.

After that, we went to a cold place that I didn't like it. It was lonely, windy, and sad. I noticed a box near us, resting on the ground near a deep hole. A man stood off a bit and was holding a shovel. Mama went to the box. She laid over that box and wailed like I had never heard before. Aunt Anya and Papa had to force her to move. The priest was there; he was talking and talking but I didn't listen. He called Peter and I over to and told us to say goodbye. That was when I realized our Rosie, our potato baby, was in that box. There was no blanket, no warm clothes, and she had no shoes.

I severely objected, "It was too cold for her! Papa! Mama always keeps her warm!" No one said anything at all to me; I had that pinching feeling in my stomach. Peter was wiping tears off his face and he took my hand in his.

The priest said something we couldn't hear over the wind; and they took the little box a bit further from us. My heart was in my throat and my stomach was pinching so much, I was afraid I might be sick. I wanted to yell and ask where our Rosie was going but I couldn't even talk. Mama was just wailing and wailing. Papa was holding her, and Aunt Anya was stroking her hair. No one was stopping them from taking Rosie. Then, that little box was lowered into the ground.

I hated them all for this. They left Rosie in the cold—they left her with no blankets and no warmth. Rosie our soft potato baby, was too little to climb out from that deep, dark hole. I hated it and I feared it. I never wanted to end up cold in the ground and left behind in the cold.

Papa

After Rosie's funeral, life was different. Peter and I played quietly, and Mama did everything slowly without talking very often. My papa, who had always been loud and boisterous, was quieter.

I admired my papa more than anything. His entire being filled our house. He was loud, he was handsome, he was everything a papa should be. Hard work and hard living never diminished his dreams and his bigger than life character. After Rosie died, a shadow fell over our home and even over Papa. He was quieter, and I suspected it was for our mama.

"Kiedy's, my Katarzyna, I will make enough to give you what you deserve. You are my beautiful aniol sent from heaven," he spoke softly to our mother, treating her as if she were made of glass.

He was a miner and looked the part with his broad shoulders. He loved the mountains and fresh air on his face. It was only when I was much older, I realized the great sacrifice he made to chase his dreams. His days were spent beneath ground, with no wind in his face and no trees. It was dark, confined, and dangerous. I never heard him complain.

Instead, he entertained our family with stories of his youth. He too had grown up in the mountains and loved fishing. I thought him invincible. He could fix things and pick my brother and I up at the same time. He could make our mama smile even on the coldest, darkest nights. We all believed him, everyone believed him, when he promised us a good future. We dreamed alongside him. His desires and dreams were infectious like a fungus; once they took hold, we never got rid of them.

That is why Mama followed him, leaving most of her family behind. She never complained about our small house or the cold winters. She simply tidied up our small house every day and cooked our simple meals as if she were preparing for a king's homecoming. Mama and Papa never placed any demands on each other but they lived for the other. They lived as if there was no doubt all their dreams would come true.

Our house was a happy, safe place. Our family was not so unlike that of everyone else we knew. Everyone was poor in our town, hoping their hard work would pay off big. We never knew we were poor or how little we had because we were the same as everyone else; it was all I knew. Life was fine until Rosie died, until reality dug its cruel claws deep into our home.

Reality was a terrifying force and laid waste to those it found in its path. It brought cold and hunger. It stole hope. Sometimes, we saw it in one of our neighbors.

Neighbors always shared on our street. We shared food and stories from home. Reality would visit a home, and then sharing was stopped. Those victims retreated inside their homes, inside themselves. Not long after, they would leave, and we would never hear from them again.

Even after Rosie and the terrible reality of leaving our baby potato in the cold ground, my papa refused to give up. He refused to allow reality too strong a grip on our home. He worked harder than ever, and I noticed he held our mother more. No matter how hard he worked or how brightly he dreamed, we found that even Papa could not keep reality away forever.

Not long after burying Rosie, we heard Papa coughing one night. He coughed deep, and it scared all of us.

He coughed and gagged all night long. I could hear him. Peter was awake all night right alongside me, but we never spoke. We were too afraid. We heard Mama bustling around, arranging cold cloths on our papa's face. She boiled the kettle and whispered all night. I am not sure how, but I knew this was bad. Mama couldn't hide her fear; she prayed and begged our Papa to "hold on" all through the night. Peter and I heard it all.

When the sun came up, Peter and I left our bed. Tiptoeing to our parents' bed, I grew afraid of a silence that hadn't been present all night. Mama was no longer whispering her prayers and Papa was no longer coughing. Complete silence.

A terrible sight befell our eyes. We knew he was dead. Death has a look. We watched Rosie lose her pinkness and slowly turn cold and blue. I could tell our Papa was gone. He was cold and blue. His shirt was covered in the blood he had coughed up all night. Mama was covered in his blood, too. It was splashed on her apron and through her hair. It was dried in specks on her face. There was blood on the blankets on their bed.

Mama was awake. She sat looking at our papa. She didn't notice us and didn't seem to see all the blood. She just stared at him as if she was trying to remember him forever. His face was relaxed and unshaven. His eyes and mouth were horribly opened, unmoving and unblinking. His mouth was circled in blood and each nostril had dried blood over it. As Peter and I looked and looked, that horrible pinching feeling in my stomach stole over my body.

Without Papa, what would happen to us? Where would we go? If Papa was not working in the mines, we could not keep this house. We would have to leave and go somewhere. Peter grasped my hand and whispered, "Mama?"

The word seemed to wake her. She stretched her thin arms wide and we rushed in, all of us crying together. Mama's thin body shook with her sobbing, there was nothing any of us could do. Papa—our worker, our storyteller, our dreamer—was lying dead in his own blood and would never be up again. Mama finally let us go. She reached over and gently closed Papa's eyes with her thin fingers. She wiped all the blood from his face. Every few seconds, his left eye would open again. It refused to stay shut. I wished it would.

She moved the blankets away from our papa and undressed him. I could tell what a hard time she had when she redressed him. When she finally got the shirt on him, she folded his arms across his chest. She closed the one eye again, but it still wouldn't stay shut. Finally, she combed his curly hair.

We watched, in silence, as she changed her own clothes and washed her own face. She never said anything to us the whole while she worked. Then, she left. There was no breakfast and no reminders to dress ourselves. Peter emptied the chamber pot, and I sat on our chair watching. Fear never left me, our new reality whispering in my ear.

We were left with our dead father, but we were not afraid. We never went to the bedside but we also did not try to look away. Instead, we studied his death. We were quiet and hungry and hardly spoke to each other. We watched Papa with his one eye staring, without seeing, at the ceiling and waited for our mother to return.

A knock at our door startled us both. Never had we been home alone when a visitor approached. We didn't know what to do, so the pounding continued. Peter and I were very frightened of whomever knocked on our door. We hid beneath the table, hoping they would just go away. They finally did. As we crawled out of our hiding place, I checked on Papa. There were no changes there.

Peter took the chair, and I climbed onto our bed. I was really getting hungry when the front door burst open. There stood our Aunt Anya. I had never been so happy to see her. She was loud, she was crying, bossing us around, and I loved her for it.

She went to our father's bed and prayed, too loudly, much louder than our mama had prayed. She tried to close his eye. It opened again. Then, she went to our stove and began heating water. She made us thick porridge, not quite as good as our mother's and told us to sit and eat.

"You can have all of it. I already had my breakfast, and your father doesn't need it. Your mother is too busy to eat, so just eat, eat all of it. Death makes the living hungry."

She was right. Peter and I were hungry. It was hot porridge that seemed to feed more than only empty bellies. As we ate, the pinching feeling of reality left me a little. For a little while, all was well in our home. We were just eating in our own home with our aunt and papa. I didn't know it was my last meal in our home or our last meal with Papa. Like most nearly five-year-old boys, I ate to eat and didn't know much about anything else. When I finished, I checked on Papa. He was still there, his one eye opened.

Aunt Anya was busy again. She was doing the dishes and folding our blankets. She opened our one suitcase on our bed. "Gather your things, all of them," she told us firmly. We didn't think to question her.

We simply gathered our things. Each of us had the following each: one nightshirt, two pairs of socks, a pair of long underwear, a pair of regular underwear, an extra shirt, and an extra pair of short pants each. They all matched, but Peter's were larger. She finished folding and was putting Mama's few possessions into the case.

All of a sudden, I realized what was happening and the pinching feeling came back deep in my stomach again. I could tell Peter understood as well—his eyes were furrowed and he was quiet. We handed her everything we could reach. The two pots, three bowls, two cups, and three spoons all went in. There was a knife and wooden spoon, a plate, a hot pad, and finally, the kettle. The kettle wouldn't fit, so Aunt Anya asked me to carry it. As Peter and I finished, we looked around. I wished we could say goodbye to the boys next door, but Aunt Anya bundled us into our coats. She bundled our blankets into our arms, and we left. We didn't even say goodbye to our papa, but I glanced back. He was there, unchanged, his one eye stuck open. Aunt Anya had taken his blanket. He looked cold and stiff. Reality was back with me, extending long fingers towards my soul. I was grateful for the cold air against my face as I followed Aunt Anya away from our home.

It seemed like we walked forever. My arms soon ached with carrying my load. Aunt Anya was not unkind but she was in a hurry. She had her own family to look after and had been away long enough.

We hurried after her, splashing through muddied streets, wondering where Mama was. The world hadn't stopped like our Papa had. The sky was blue and clear. Horses pulled their wagons. People went about their usual daily business. I saw a group of kids playing and I wished I was with them. I wished Papa was working in the mine.

About halfway to Aunt Anya's home, I noticed a large, white cat following us. Her fur was full and dirty. She had big blue eyes that reminded me of Rosie's. One ear was scarred. Something had taken a bite out of it. Her tail stood up straight, but the end bent at a ninety-degree angle. The cat never left me the whole way to Aunt Anya's.

My arms felt as if they would fall off. I was sure my legs were going to crumble before we stopped walking. We finally reached our aunt's house, legs and arms intact. It was nearly identical to ours. Inside here were two beds, a chair, a stove, and a table with a bench. There were even two children, though they were younger than Peter and I.

We went inside. Aunt Anya piled our things into a corner and gathered all four of us children to her. "Your father has died. There is nothing for you here, so now, your mother has gone to look for work. You have no money. You cannot stay in that house. I cannot afford to feed you for long because, you see, we also have no money. I want to help but I can only do a little. Peter and Jurak, you will stay with us for a few days while Katarzyna looks for her work, then you will go with her." She crossed herself while she told us this. Peter and I only nodded. We understood our new reality.

Papa was dead. We were on our own.

The Flop House

After a few days, I realized it was not so nice to be at Aunt Anya's house. Peter complained we were treated like babies. Plus, we had to share a bed with our cousins. They kicked all night. Aunt Anya looked at us and cried so often, I began to wonder if Peter and I were sick like Rosie and Papa. I didn't feel sick and I never heard Peter cough, but that pinching feeling in my stomach was a constant companion.

Every night, I dreamt of cold holes in the ground that were full of blank staring eyes. I wondered if Peter dreamt like me but I was too afraid and never asked him. I never told anyone about those dreams either. I never told how much they frightened me. I felt Aunt Anya was too busy, and there was no one else to tell.

We stayed and stayed, never knowing where Mama was or how she was doing. Knowing where our Papa was didn't ease our fears. Aunt Anya did her best to make us feel better. She cooked a lot and bossed us around all day. We obeyed her every command. We washed our hands and behind our ears. We cleaned our plates. She loved us the best way she knew. She kept us safe and clean. I guessed she didn't think to explain where Mama went.

We lived in a mining camp nestled into the foothills of the Big Horn Mountains. The houses were all the same, neatly lined up in neat rows along straight but muddy roads. It was at once both minimal and overcrowded. Every type of person in the world seemed to reside in our little corner of the world. We heard Chinese, Irish, Scotch, Polish, German, and Russian daily. There was one general store that sold everything from fabric to dried goods. Everyone called it a camp but Papa had promised it would become a real town. I never thought we would leave; it had everything we ever wanted.

Just south of the camp was a real wild-west boomtown called Sheridan, Wyoming. The trolley that connected all the camps initiated there. The main street was lined with luxurious shops selling the latest fashions seen in New York City. Humble general stores dotted the side streets. It was ten times bigger than any other town fifty miles in every direction. Horses and noise filled the streets. Peter and I loved the trolley car best of all.

Our mama had gone to Sheridan in search of work. Despite having no education or savings, she found work in one of the four flophouses. We found out, much later, that Mama was hired on the spot for housekeeping. She had started immediately, and it was a good job. It gave her a small wage, plus room and board. It took her nearly a month to save enough to come collect Peter and I. We never heard from her during that entire time.

When she finally appeared in Aunt Anya's doorway, I was so happy to see her. That pinching in my stomach stopped pinching quite as hard with one hug. She was beautiful as ever even though she looked a little tired. Aunt Anya fussed around, taking up too much space. It was hard to get to Mama but finally, Mama pushed past Anya. She sat on one of the chairs. Peter wrapped his arms around her shoulders, and I was pulled into her lap. The three of us sat for a long while, happily holding on to one another. It was just us now. No Papa and no Rosie. Just us three, alone, unwanted by the rest of the world.

Aunt Anya generously let us stay one more night. The three of us took one bed, and Aunt Anya's family took the other. Peter slept on Mama's right, and I to her left. We wrapped ourselves in our blankets, and Mama sang in her soft way, lulling us to sleep. The next morning, Aunt Anya and Mama cooked us breakfast and held a whispered conversation in the corner kitchen

"Is this really the only way, Katarzyna? Is there nowhere else?" Aunt Anya loudly whispered. I did not think she really knew how to whisper.

"This is all I can find; it is not too bad, not as bad as it sounds. I will be serving the customers food, nothing else. In between, I will have the wash. There is shelter and it is near the school. What more can I ask for? I can't mine and stay here. Jurak and Peter will be safer than here, alone all day. At least there, I will be near them. We can't stay here. The money has run out, this is it," Mama choked on the last words even as she straightened her back with hard resolve.

Her sister reached a hand to her hand, "I wish we had never left Istebna, Katarazyna; I wish we had never left Cziesyn! I am so sorry I fell in love," I had never seen Aunt Anya cry, not even when our Rosie died. She spilled a lifetime of tears that wet her face and our mama's shoulder.

"Hush, Anya. This is not your fault. You love your Antonin as I love my Petr. As I loved my Petr. This is precious, dar milosci. Petr is now gone, but your Antonin is here alive and well. Be thankful. Sheridan is not too far."

Aunt Anya seemed to agree even though her shoulders shook.

"I have buried Petr near Rosie but I cannot afford to mark his grave. I am so afraid he will lie here, forgotten. It is my greatest sadness. Visit them, will you?" One lone tear found its way down her cheek. Mama brushed it aside, then squared her shoulders and called us boys. We dutifully hugged our Aunt Anya and cousins. We gathered our few belongings and followed Mama through the front door.

The street was dirty, as always, and busy. The vile stench of horses and men reached our senses. Peter and I wrinkled our noses against it. I tried to be brave, but it was hard to keep up with my arms full. The pinching feeling came back deep in my stomach. I knew we were going to the big town and I was scared. I looked around looking for something to help me through this change, but no one noticed us—they were just too busy with their own lives filled with their own worries. I began to wish for anyone to notice us, to have time to care just a little. As we reached the trolley car, I saw that white cat again. I was sure it was the same one so I called out for her to come to me. My wish had been granted. She came. Just as we were pulling away, she jumped into the seat next to me. We became fast friends by the time we got to Sheridan. I had named her Rosa. I don't think Mama even noticed.

The ride to Sheridan was not long but, for me, very exciting. The wind whipped up around us. Dead leaves rushed around. Rosa was perturbed by those and glared. Birds flew overhead. Peter, always adventurous, dared to look over the side down at the track. Mama pulled him back with a sharp word.

Sheridan was huge. I was afraid of getting lost as we disembarked the trolley. It clanged away, leaving us in the street alone. Mama knew where to go. She hurried us both along. People jostled us this way and that way, so I kept close to Mama.

I felt we walked along ways, but it was probably only three or four city blocks. Mama finally stopped in front of a large, white building. It was the biggest building I had ever seen. We stood in front of the main door. Windows stretched right and left. It was taller than any other building around. Mama bustled us inside without looking around. She didn't bother to explain why we were there.

Even without explanation, we followed her, dutifully, down a narrow hall that was filled with people. They were everywhere. They leaned against walls, sprawled in doorways and two men were passed out beneath a low window. Shouts and laughter rose up from somewhere down to the right. Loud piano music followed. Peter glanced at me, his eyes wide. Mama took us far down that narrow hall. We followed her up the narrow stairs where more people were gathered. A few sat on the stairs and were unwilling to move out of our way. We climbed awkwardly around each one. One lady winked at me. She had short dark hair and wore a light pink dress with no sleeves and a long, tight skirt. Her skin was deep brown. I had never seen a black woman before and I couldn't help but stare. I thought she was beautiful. Later, I learned she was called Miss Kate.

Mama led us up another flight of stairs. We walked down another long hallway. Finally, pulling a large key from her apron pocket, she stopped in front of a door. She let us in first and shut the door firmly behind her. She finally spoke.

"This will be our home, at least for now. I will work in the restaurant and you boys will behave. The man who owns this place is doing us a favor. His name is Mr. Joclav. He doesn't want any trouble from children."

Peter and I hadn't been paying much attention to her words. We were too busy exploring our new living quarters. I was terribly frightened. Peter looked unwell. The noise was loud, even with the door shut and locked. The window only shut part way.

Beside the window and door, there was one small bed with no blankets. The stand was of iron and it held a thin, stained mattress. I could see a chamber pot beneath it. In one corner, there stood a washbasin with no pitcher. There was a strip of wood nailed haphazardly into the wall next to the washbasin. There were three hooks on it. Mama hung our coats on those. Other than a distinct musty smell, the room was empty.

Mama was talking again.

"Listen, Peter, Jurak. This is very important. You must behave. This is the only place in town that allows us to stay. I can find work but nowhere to live. Do you understand? You stay out of the way of everyone here and you stay out of trouble. Mr. Joclav has given me a job and this place to rent. We can eat dinners from the restaurant, but you must behave. He would rather you not stay and if he never sees you, he will be happiest. Do you understand?" Her voice was low and urgent.

I nodded slowly. I wondered when and if Peter and I had behaved badly. Were we as loud as all these people in this place? Had we been impolite to someone? Peter dropped his eyes to the floor. "I miss Papa."

It was the first time any of the three of us acknowledged our new life with our new, lonely circumstances. Mama pulled us to her and even though we were all a little hungry, we curled up on that bed together. We cried ourselves to sleep. Despite all the noise and the newness, we slept deeply. We slept right through dinner and the whole night through. When Peter and I woke the next morning, Mama was already gone.

There was new water in our kettle. Mama placed it by the basin the day before. Peter made me wash after he did his. Then, he opened our door and we peered out into the hallway. It was quiet. I couldn't believe it was the same hallway—it was so quiet. Besides one man sleeping down towards the stairs, it was also empty. There was no shouting, no laughing, and no piano music. Peter led me towards the stairs and we tiptoed down in search of our mother.

The smell of food hit both of us as soon as we reached the bottom of those stairs. I took a good look around and took in our new home as we walked. There were many doors that were all the same. Some closed better than others. The smell of food grew strong the more we walked. Peter took a sharp right at the bottom of the stairs. Another long hallway greeted us, so we trekked down it too. There, at the end, was the restaurant and our mother. I was relieved to see both.

Mama looked happy to see us too. She beckoned us in with a quick glance over her shoulder. She pulled bread from her front apron pocket and kissed us both. We sat there, by the backdoor of the kitchen waiting to see what we were to do next. She came to us with a glass full of milk and told us to share.

"This is where I work," she proclaimed a bit proudly. "I know how to cook and clean, and Mr. Joclav will let us stay as long as we need. This kitchen is busy all the time, especially at night. I worked before I had you boys. I worked in a kitchen in Czsien. I will work every day, and you boys are in charge of yourselves. You must be good and kind. You can start school soon."

"School?" Peter asked this question and his brows furrowed. We had never gone to school before. He didn't sound too happy.

"Yes, school. You will learn to read better and do math and when you grow up, you will not be miners. Now run along, and I will see you at dinner time here." Mama waved us out the door even though I still felt a little hungry.

Peter ran through the kitchen door without asking for more, so I followed, hot on his heels. Almost immediately, Peter crashed into something big and hard, and I crashed into him. We fell in a heap at the feet of a really big man. We untangled ourselves and looked up to see who had stopped us so suddenly. The man did not look kind.

He had greasy hair that slicked away from his face. His shirt was unwashed, and he smelled. He looked down at us, his big mouth stretching into a slimy smile. I didn't like him. I looked at my brother and could see he didn't like him either.

"You boys must belong to Katarzyna. Did you eat breakfast?" His voice was loud and his breath horrible. I decided to let Peter do the talking.

"Yes, sir, we ate breakfast with Mama just now," Peter sounded like a grown-up. I was awed by his sure steady words.

"Good then, you run along and stay out of the way, you hear? You have your room here and your mother has her job, but you boys stay out of the way." His eyes narrowed and his fists doubled. Peter and I stepped around him and ran to the end of the alleyway without looking back. Rosa was waiting for me.

Peter ran far ahead leaving me to keep up. Rosa followed, right on my heels. When Peter came to the end of the city block, he stopped. I crashed into him for the second time that morning. I fell and scraped my hands and knees. I tried not to let him see the tears in my eyes. I looked up and saw why he had stopped so suddenly.

The street was just as busy as yesterday. No one was going to watch out for us. It would be up to us to watch out for *them*. Peter slowed a little after that, leading me up streets and alleys we had never been down. He never seemed to get lost. We spent the entire day getting to know the town. We found it all exciting.

Finally, night began to fall, and Peter led us home. The street was still busy and people were getting louder. Many called to each other and we saw a fight start outside one saloon. An Indian tried to go inside but he was shoved out immediately. He shoved back until someone gave him a drink.

We entered the large building through the backdoor into the kitchen. Mama was nowhere to be found, but a smiley, brown woman greeted us.

"Where ya boys headed?" she asked in a faint eastern accent.

"We live here, and Mama said we can get our dinner here. We don't know where she is." Peter followed that simple explanation with, "I am Peter, and this is Jurak." I was too afraid to answer. She was the most beautiful woman I had ever seen.

Summer and School

Her hair was black and short, cut just to her jaw. She wore a light dress covered with an apron. Obviously, she worked in the kitchen with our mama. She had wide green eyes, fringed with long dark lashes. I could tell she smiled a lot—her soft features easily stretched upwards, wrinkling her eyes. She had soft looking hands with long, supple fingers. She smiled at us.

"You belong to Kat! I was hoping to meet you soon. Your mama is busy out front, so I will get your dinner to you today. You boys can call me Kate," she called to us, over her shoulder as she walked away. She talked with a New York accent.

She returned a few minutes later, carrying a large tray. To mine and Peter's surprise, there was another glass of milk! We had never had two glasses of milk in one day. Alongside that milk, there was a large piece of bread and two bowls of a thick soup. Peter and I ate hurriedly while Miss Kate told us all about our new home.

"There are four floors. Tons of people move in and out every day. We see all kinds and the rich people stay on the fourth floor. Did your mama warn you about the owner?" She dropped her voice to a serious whisper. "He is the big man they call him Mr. Joclav. I try to stay out of his way and you should too. I never saw him harm anybody, but he can be cruel. I saw him toss a girl into the street over an unpaid bill. You stay out of his way and you'll be fine. I been here for nearly two years! I came out thinking I would keep going to California, you know? But I only made it here so far; I'll keep goin' someday. For now, I do the dishes here and a bit of side work on the weekends. You boys seen the trolley yet? I can get you a ride tomorah if you like. You never know who you gonna meet out there, and riding is fun." The more she talked, the more I liked her. Her accent seemed exotic and her eyes were kind. She went on, "What'd you boys see today?"

I was no longer so afraid of her. "We saw the trolley, and Peter took me and Rosa all over!"

Peter chimed in, "We saw the streets and all the people, Jurak liked the shop windows! I liked the horses."

"Who's Rosa, hun?"

I hadn't talked to anyone too much about Rosa just yet. Peter had noticed her following us, but I hadn't told him what I called her. I hadn't told Mama about her either.

"She's my cat. She likes to see this city and she just likes me. She followed us from home." I could see Miss

Kate could tell how much I loved Rosa, so I continued, "She is really fluffy and has blue eyes, like me!"

"She sounds neat, maybe I can see her tomorah? We can bring her a bite to eat. I never had a cat before, will she bite?" she teased.

Mama came in just then, and Peter and I ran to her. I felt like we hadn't seen her for longer than just today. She hugged us close and asked Miss Kate to get her some soup. Peter asked for more too. I expected Mama to admonish him—we never got two bowls of anything before—but she didn't. I immediately wished I had thought to ask for more.

"Tell me of your day, boys." Mama was so soft and gentle. Peter talked and talked about our day. I was tired, so I just let Peter talk and snuggled into Mama. Kate brought our tray back. She touched my cheek before walking away, and I happily noticed she had included another bowl of soup for me even though I hadn't asked. I loved her more and more.

Peter talked and talked to Mama, telling her of all the people and how Miss Kate promised us a trolley ride. He never mentioned Rosa and was content to just eat and listen. Mama seemed awfully tired, and I noticed her hands were very red. She ate her soup in silence, but her eyes looked happy to see us.

Afterwards, she took our tray away and was gone for a few minutes.

Retrieving us, she led the way up to our room. "It is bath night, we get to bathe once a week in the tub down the hall," she informed us as we walked. "We get Mondays which is best; hardly anyone else has that day—it will be cleaner."

We got to our room, and Mama gathered our washing things. She had a bar of soap, a comb that pulled too much, a threadbare towel that scratched a lot, and clean clothes for all three of us. I was not so sure about bathing here. Someone might walk in or the water might be cold. Peter looked as if he held the same reservations, but Mama was determined. "I don't want to sleep with smelly boys again!"

We always obeyed our mama, so we followed her down the stairs and down another hall. There were people all around again, noisily strewn all over the halls. We picked our way around them and continued into a room labeled WASH.

Mama closed the door firmly behind us, and I was relieved to see a latch. I hadn't noticed Mama bring our weekly wash with her on top of all our bathing things.

"Mondays are our wash days, clothes and all," she informed us. She went to work, filling an iron tub with water from a pump. Peter and I took turns when her arms grew tired.

When it was full, Mama put all our linens into the water. There was a washboard to the side, and she took it down, bar of soap in one hand and Peter's socks in the other. Washing clothes was a lot of work, and we had two blankets besides clothing she wanted cleaned. Peter and I took all our clothes off and helped wet the clothes and soap them. Mama made it fun, splashing us here and there and scrubbing our backs in between.

Soon, we were both wet and cold and dripping with suds. Peter painted a beard to my face with the suds, and we all laughed. It felt good. Once our laundry was done, Mama wrung it out and bundled it into a wet sheet. She stepped out of her clothes into the tub and Peter and I helped each other dry off. She was thinner than I remembered, her ribs sticking far out of her back and sides. She washed best as she could in water left from us and the wash. She finally rinsed her hair and Peter brought her our damp towel.

She drew her dressing gown around her shoulders and we gathered our things. We traced our steps back to our room where Mama hung a cord diagonally from corner to corner, and we handed her the wet laundry. Soon, our room smelled fresh just like our soap. Mama lay down in the middle of our bed and the three of us snuggled in close together.

"The first time I saw your Papa, I knew he loved me," her words were soft. "You both know he was a large man, hard to miss, but I noticed his eyes first. I knew he was watching me at the market that day. I wondered if he would get enough courage to speak to me, to say hello. He was loud, you know how loud he was. I think I loved him from that moment. He didn't even have to say anything."

Her voice caught at those words and she didn't say anything more. I felt her arm tighten on me, holding me as safe as she could. Noises from all around filled our ears and minds, eventually lulling us to sleep.

The Cost of Warmth

Peter and I did just as we'd planned. We left home each morning and went onto school. At noon, we simply walked out of the schoolyard. Ms. Fink never asked and no one else cared. School was tolerable as long as we didn't ruin entire days with it.

Once we settled into our rhythm, I noticed the days quickly grew cooler. Most nights were cold enough that we could see our breath as we snuggled under our blankets.

"It is getting too cold in this room," Mama spoke after washing one night. "I am afraid our things won't dry. They will just freeze in the winter." Mama looked worried. Peter watched her with a serious look. All three of us understood only too well what cold could do to a body. Mama sighed and looked over our things. I think she was noticing how worn out our shoes were and how small Peter's jacket was for him. I didn't want to worry her so much just by growing and I hugged her tight. She kissed the top of my head and told me I smelled clean. I felt better but I wasn't sure Mama did.

After school the next day, Peter asked if we shouldn't save some of our pennies for Mama instead of spending it on our sweets. Peter pointed out my shoes were worn through. His shoes were worn through at the toe and his arms stuck far past the sleeves of his coat. We had to give up our candy.

Throughout the next few weeks, we were able to save twelve cents. Mama couldn't hold her tears back when we presented her with our savings. She clung to us and her shoulders shook. Peter and I were amazed at her emotion. After all, we were busy each day with school and our afternoon adventures, we couldn't have known too much of our mother's day or what a family like ours costs. That night, though she didn't use words, Peter and I felt that biting reality deep in our stomachs again. Mama never shared her daily struggles with us, but we knew how hard she worked. She began each day before sun up and finished well after dark. Her arms were strong from all the washing she did but she was thin from lack of food. Dark circles framed her eyes, and her clothes grew thinner by the day.

Mama faced her own demons of worry and stress knowing there was little more we could do to free us of our desperate situation. She never complained but she had to be lonely. Sheridan was a fine, booming city in the north, but her only family lived far enough away that we never saw them. She made friends with the other women at work and never deviated from her daily tasks. She had no other choice but simply to wake and work each day. No one hugged her fears or worries away and no one shared her concerns.

One night, an especially cold night, I noticed Mama looking around our room. Her eyes hardened. She knew we would not survive in such cold all winter. She clung to us that night and I felt safer than ever, just by her touch. I could hear Rosa, just outside our window, purring away, my brother breathing so deeply, and my heart was content as it could be. My belly was full of food and even though we all missed our old life very much, I found contentment that night.

The day after, it was a Tuesday, and we saw the first frost covering the ground on our way to school. Miss Kate served our breakfast and we could taste the extra sugar she had added to our porridge. She even warmed our milk.

After breakfast, we walked quickly to school even though we were not excited to sit all morning. Ms. Fink was stern but nice. We just didn't want to sit. I was happy with my learning though. I was reading better and my math skills were improving. Ms. Fink had complimented me just yesterday on my hard work.

It was a fine day, hard and cold. Thankfully, the sun was shining and warmed the earth a little. Peter and I hurried up to our school and through the door and found our seats. Peter hadn't said a word the entire way, he looked deep in thought, and Rosa and I didn't bother him.

After school, Peter and I ran to check our traps. We had only one rabbit. It was too cold to swim so I led Peter to the best fishing spot. Peter marveled at my talent for fishing. I always caught the most and all we used were sticks with a bit of twine and a homemade hook. I couldn't explain how I knew where the fish were or just when to yank them out of the water. I just knew, the same way Rosa knew.

We slowly walked back to town, we would sell our rabbit, but there wouldn't be candy today and our fishing trip hadn't lasted that long. Most of the trees had lost their leaves already. Peter was still very quiet, and I had that funny pinching feeling in my stomach but I couldn't explain why.

We walked by Smith's, but Victoria was helping customers, so she didn't see us. Peter seemed gloomier than ever; the dark sky matched our mood. Rosa was the only one who was untroubled of us three; she had her fish and happily trotted behind us.

We reached the kitchen door and went in only to run into Mr. Joclav. He looked greasier than ever, "Boys!" he boomed, glaring out into the street behind us, I was scared he saw Rosa, "How was your learning today? You don't want to let your mother down. She worked hard for you today," he sneered and walked away. Miss Kate was there to take our fish and she watched him go, her eyes narrowing as he stomped through the kitchen.

"I'll take these," she said, taking the fish from hand. "You boys stay outta his way—he's in a mean one tonight. I'll take care of your dinner and eat with ya. We can talk about our day." She seemed worried, quieter than normal and ignored us when we asked about our mother.

That pinching feeling was in my stomach again. I had no idea why I felt that way, so I checked on Rosa. She was there, safely eating her fish. When I shut the door, I saw Mr. Joclav, watching from across the kitchen and, this time, I knew he had seen Rosa. He leaned against the wall and put his hands in his pants pockets, narrowing his eyes at me. Peter was very strong and ignored him even though I knew he was wondering why Mr. Joclav was suddenly so interested in us. We had never had the misfortune of running into him since our first day here.

Miss Kate took a long while, longer than normal, getting our dinner. I could hear Peter's stomach over mine which was loudly demanding food. Mr. Joclav watched us the entire time with focused eyes, daring us to make some sort of trouble. Finally, I heard Miss Kate's small quick steps returning and Mr. Joclav silently walked away. She also noticed Mr. Joclav leave. Mama remained absent from the kitchen.

Miss Kate finally brought our tray over and quietly said, "I'll be eating with ya boys tonight. We will go to your mother in just a little while, she's restin' right now. Tell me about school." She said all this in her usual New York accent but much slower and quieter than normal and she never met our eyes. Peter looked at me very worried, we had never known Mama to rest.

"Where is Mama then, in our room?" Peter's voice was authoritative, even demanding. I had never heard him speak to an adult like that before. I looked to Miss Kate, and when she didn't answer, I looked back to him. Peter stared very hard at Miss Kate, willing her to answer.

Looking to the food, she said, "Peter, Jurak, I will help you and I will help your mother, but, for now, let's just eat. Then, I will take you to her." Peter looked very angry and I knew my own eyes were wide with fear.

Miss Kate pointed to our food, willing us not to argue. We ate, but I hardly tasted the food that night. Miss Kate tried to rally us around, she remarked on how good our fish tasted and how soft the bread was. We didn't answer, and I wondered what Mama would eat.

Finally, Miss Kate took our tray away and we watched as she scrubbed each dish. None of us noticed Mr. Joclav return. Miss Kate started when she turned around and saw his dark outline against the wall. Her hand went to her heart. He liked scaring her like that. He didn't say a word nor stop us when she led us from the kitchen. Miss Kate led us to the second floor and to the left. We had never been to this part of the building before. It was still full of people but felt warmer than our own hallway. Peter pointed out we were right above the kitchen and going the wrong way to our room.

"Mr. Joclav moved you today, and your new room is over this way. Your mother is already there," Miss Kate explained. I wondered why she hadn't said this before;

after all, a move was a big deal. Then, I wondered why we were moved.

"Well, why didn't you tell us before now? Why didn't Mama wait for us to help her? We ain't got much, but it took all three of us carrying it here." Again, Peter sounded much older than his years, and again Miss Kate ignored him. My stomach pinched tight again.

She led us down to the very end, proving Peter was right; we were right above the kitchen—I could hear the clatter of dishes. Miss Kate softly knocked on our new door and opened it about halfway.

The room looked much like our other one. There was a bed and a window, but this one had something metal beneath the window. I didn't know what it was. I looked back around to the bed looking for our mama.

Mama was lying in our bed, and Miss Vicki was sitting near her. She was speaking low and gently to our mama.

"Just a bit more, Kat, just a bit more, then you can rest. Kate took care of your boys, and they're here now, nice and warm."

"Joclav," muttered our mother, so low we could hardly hear as she ate a bit more from the offered spoon. Miss Vicki stood up. She looked us over and thanked Miss Kate who left quickly.

"Your mama is a little bit sick, but she will be better in a few days. In the meantime, I will take care of her. You boys need to behave extra good. I found her trying to carry your belongings outside your old door.

She was in a state, but I cleaned her up best as I could. She was worried about you two but hasn't really told me what happened. She is in pain. Thankfully, there are no broken bones."

Miss Vicki's voice became even quieter and more serious, Peter and I leaned in to hear what she was saying. "Now, you two stay out of Mr. Joclav's way, no matter what your mama says in her sleep or in this fever. Promise me you will stay away from him. If you see him in your hall, don't look too much at him. If he talks, look down and nod. Answer if you must but please, stay away from him." She was wiping her cheeks as she spoke.

We looked over to our mama. Her forehead was wet and her hair swept away from her face, she was shivering even in the blankets and our room warm as it was. Instinctively, I looked out the window for Rosa, how would she know of our move? She was there, though I never understood how she'd knew where to find us.

I heard Peter begin to cry as he asked what happened to our mama. I looked closer, her face was bruised all over and her lip was badly cut with eye was swollen completely shut. Miss Vicki explained, "Perhaps she fell down the stairs as she tried to move your things. I am just not sure. I have taken care of her though and I swear she will be fine in just a few days. Let her rest and if she needs anything, you come find me. Now promise me once more, you will stay away from Mr. Joclav, no matter what." I glanced at Peter who was already nodding, so I nodded too. Miss Vicki left.

There was nothing for Peter and me to do. We carefully climbed into the bed next to our poor mother. Instead of her wrapping us in her arms, we wrapped ours around her. I put my hand ever so softly to her cheek and whispered, "I love you, Mama." I don't know if she heard me or not because she never answered.

The morning light made her face look even worse. We were unused to waking with her next to us and we were a bit unsure what to do. Her one eye opened a crack and she said, "You boys run along to school; I will be better by the time you get back." I didn't want to leave her, but Peter was already kissing her cheek goodbye. I looked to the window and saw Rosa sitting there in the sun. I could see the frost behind her but our room was very warm.

I followed Peter down the stairs and to the kitchen. Miss Kate seemed to be back to normal and fussed over our breakfast. I could taste the sugar again. She patted me on my head as Peter and I left. This time, Rosa didn't follow us to school. I didn't have to wonder why—I knew she was watching over Mama.

Even with Mama unwell, Peter and I left the schoolyard at noon to fish and check our traps. Our traps were full, which seemed to brighten Peter's day. We would get two pennies today for our work. I hoped Peter would buy at least one piece of candy but wasn't sure. I knew he was trying to save for at least one pair of shoes. We caught three good-sized fish and headed back a little earlier than our normal time. Rosa stayed away the entire time.

Peter led the way to the old woman who paid him, happy to see our good catch. I didn't notice until I heard the trolley that we hadn't gone by Smith's. I wasn't too disappointed even though root beer candy had sounded good all day. I wanted to check on our mother.

Rosa was at the kitchen door waiting to greet me. I gave her part of my fish since I hadn't caught her one of her own. I patted her while she purred her thanks. I loved her so much and even more for watching our mama that day. Peter took the fish from me and went inside. I stayed outside a bit longer. I thanked Rosa softly and scratched her around the chin and ears, just the way she liked.

Miss Kate made our dinner but didn't eat with us. Instead, she kept one fish to the side, for Mama she told us and took another tray to Miss Vicki to bring to Mama. After we were finished, we left our tray, and I followed Peter to our new room on the second floor.

We could hear Miss Vicki as we got to the top of the stairs, "Leave, just leave her alone, allow her to rest and get well enough to work. Just leave." We had never heard Miss Vicki speak quite that way to anyone before and my stomach got that pinch of reality right in the pit. I knew, without seeing who she was talking to. I craned my neck and saw, without satisfaction that I'd been right. Mr. Joclav was standing outside our new door.

He towered over her and for a moment I was afraid he was going to hit her. Instead, he slowly turned and I could see he was not in a jovial mood. Miss Vicki muttered only a few words I could really hear, 'drunk' and 'bastard' as he stumbled down the hallway, right towards Peter and I. We remembered our promise to Miss Vicki the prior night and we dropped our eyes as that terrible man drew near. Peter's hands were in tight fists. When he edged by us, Mr. Joclav whispered, "Ask her. Ask her if it was worth it to make her boys warm."

Peter and I kept our promise even though we were both shaking. I was afraid and angry. I hated Mr. Joclav and I knew it was him who had hurt our mama.

Christmas

It was cold. Peter and I walked to school and were cold. The fields were cold and our fishing hole was cold. I was so cold after we left the school I wanted to go right back. Miss Fink kept that building warm. It was made warmer as the windows frosted over, creating beautiful crystals between us and the outside. Peter still led us away each day but Rosa refused to follow us out of town. I wanted to follow her home and I finally got the courage to tell Peter how I felt.

"Peter, I don't want to go every day anymore. It is too cold and besides, our traps are empty most of the time," I pointed out that last bit very logically. "We could check the traps after school once or twice a week and still pay for Mama's Christmas present. Please, Peter. Let's stop leaving the warm every single day."

Peter was cold though he never complained. He walked quickly with his hands stuffed into his pockets. He never threw snow like the other kids and he grew very angry if any was thrown at us. He drew his collar up over his face as far as it would reach and kept his head down against any breeze. He glared at my suggestion, but I made up my mind. I wasn't going every day anymore as long as it was winter.

The next day, right at noon, Peter stood up as if to leave. He looked around for me to follow but I stayed seated. He glared hard at me and headed out on his own. My stomach had that pinching feeling but I too, had made up my mind. Miss Fink watched him leave, glancing at me. Rosa didn't follow him either.

All afternoon, I worried about Peter, thinking that I should have followed him. I never walked home alone and the thought of it made me nervous. I wondered where Peter had gone while I sat and stared at my reader all afternoon. I was the first one out when Miss Fink finally released us. I was glad I was warm but it had been a long afternoon. Rosa followed at my heels and as ready as I was to find Peter.

I was surprised to find Peter waiting for me at the end of the schoolyard. He never spoke, just led the way through the fields. I loved my brother more than anything that day. It was I who abandoned him, yet he came back for me. He was a good big brother.

We checked our traps and were happy to find two rabbits. Their carcasses steamed in the cold as Peter cleaned them. We made our way to the creek and broke the thin ice that covered our fishing hole. Rosa refused to get onto the ice. I was happy it took no time at all to catch four fish. Peter cleaned those too, and I noticed their guts didn't steam like the rabbits had. Rosa licked her chops as I handed her a fish, and we took our catch back to town.

I hunkered down near the building while Peter talked to the old woman. He pocketed the coins, and we quickly walked to our building. Rosa stayed close but I could tell she wanted to run from the wind that was picking up. I wanted to run too but I was already out of breath from the cold wind. Finally, finally, we reached our building. Peter opened the backdoor, and Rosa took off. I was relieved to be home.

Mama fried our fish and, as the three of us ate, told us, "Boys, tomorrow begins your Christmas break." Peter and I had never heard of a Christmas break. Papa worked every day except Sundays, Christmas or not. In this place, Mama worked every day, even Sundays.

"Schools close for a week to celebrate the holidays. Teachers go home to see their families and since there is no teacher, no students can go either. We will go to church on Christmas Eve and Christmas morning." Peter made a face; church wasn't any better than school. I didn't make a face but I agreed with him.

It was the day before Christmas Eve and a Monday, so it was wash night. Mama told us that was good luck, everything lined up nicely for a good break, a good start to the holidays. I didn't feel like washing, though. I was tired from the cold and though our building was warm, I didn't want to get wet and cold. I followed Mama without arguing though. Peter and I never argued with her, not once in all the time since we had moved.

We scrubbed and washed till we were clean. I had been right—it was cold after washing. We helped Mama hang our wash. I got into bed, but Mama stayed out. She collected our new things and neatly lined them up for tomorrow. She brushed our coats off, making sure the wool was dust free. She wiped our shoes off with a soft cloth till they gleamed in the soft light. I fell asleep contentedly listening to her rustling around.

Christmas was a big deal in our building that year. The next morning, I followed Peter down to the kitchen then outside and up the street. We had a present to collect and we were very excited. The pin seemed prettier than when we had first found it. Victoria informed us we had change and showed us a new flavor of candy. Peter bought three.

Before we even opened that kitchen door, we could smell something amazing. Rosa didn't run away either. I had to push her back out and remind her she wasn't allowed. The kitchen was busier than normal. Miss Vicki was helping Mama and both women were smiling. Miss Kate brought us a tray and Mama joined us. Then, to our surprise, Miss Kate joined us and soon after, so did Miss Vicki.

There was so much extra food that night—a roast, potatoes, and a thick soup filled us up. Miss Kate warmed our milk, and Miss Vicki brought us each a small piece of pie. Peter filled his cheeks and gulped down most of our milk, but I didn't mind. It was the best food I ever ate. The five of us laughed and ate, taking a little longer than normal to finish our dinner.

Mama's eyes didn't look tired and she was smiling her old way with her mouth stretched wide over her teeth and eyes crinkled up. As she turned to take our tray away, she hurried Peter and me up to ready for Church. Peter stopped smiling at those words but that only made me laugh.

Miss Vicki followed us, "Wash your face and your necks. Tuck in your shirts and fold your socks." She had a long list of how to make us church presentable. It took me a long while to do all she told us. Peter hurried through but was sent back to do better. Mama finally came up and combed our hair down just right and put on her new shawl. The three of us left our room together. Mr. Joclav was blocking our way.

Peter refused to look away but I dropped my gaze. Mama put us behind her and made her way slowly but surely down the hall. I could feel her begin to shake as we grew close.

"Looking good, Kat. Your face is not so embarrassing anymore." The man had no respect for anyone or anything. Mama didn't answer, just moved around him, and hurried us to the stairs. Thankfully, he stayed in the hall just watching us go.

Miss Florence and Miss Vicki joined us, and we all marched through the extremely crowded restaurant and out the front door. A line had formed for those waiting to eat that night. I had never seen it so busy! Even with Mr. Joclav lurking around our building, I was excited and we soon forgot our troubles as we hurried by the line of men. I looked at them as we walked by, Rosa rushing between us.

They were mostly young with bright eyes talking about Christmas in their homelands. One man looked vaguely familiar and he smiled warmly at Mama as we passed by but she was too busy with us to take much of a notice. I suspected many men smiled at our beautiful Mama, she was too used to such attention and learned to ignore it. Peter noticed though and glared at the young man.

We reached the church which was busier than ever and as we hurried in, Mama reminded us to keep it quiet. We were learning about the baby Jesus again and how he changed the world.

I liked the story and I even liked the songs this year but I didn't pay too much attention. I was wondering how a small baby had managed to change the world. Our baby was gone, forgotten by all but us three. She changed our lives but no one else's and now, she was out in some field with no visitors. I saw Mama wipe a tear from her cheek and knew she was remembering our little potato too. Peter held onto Mama's hand and we all listened to the rest of the service, kneeling when Mama did and crossing ourselves as Miss Florence and Miss Vicki did. Finally, it was over.

The night was clear and cold. There was no line in front of our restaurant but it was full of everyone. We could hear them as we drew near. People were laughing and singing old songs with terrible off-key voices. Mama led us to the back. Rosa left us after I patted her and wished her a good night. She wound herself past us and to her warm home away from us.

"You stay put," Miss Florence ordered once we were in. "I have a treat for ya and I don't want to up just yet." She hurried across the kitchen, excited to retrieve the surprise. Miss Vicki followed her.

Mama sat down heavily, finally looking tired but happy. Peter joined her on her left and I on the right and the three of us held onto each other for just a little while. It felt as if the world was made of just us even as the noise from the restaurant seemed to shake the entire building. Mama hummed a Christmas song.

Miss Vicki brought Mama a small glass with amber liquid. Mama held it, waiting for Miss Florence. She finally returned with two cups, steaming and foamy. "For you, boys; bottoms up!" she proclaimed.

I tilted mine back, gasping at the warmth. It was the best thing I ever tasted. It was creamy and sweet, "Hot chocolate! Ya ever had it?" Miss Florence asked. Mama shook her head no. Peter drank deeply, almost inhaling his. I let Mama have a taste. Our little party lasted only a little longer and then we headed off to bed.

We had always celebrated Christmas, but Peter and I never had new clothes nor asked for any presents. Mama always made us a good, thick soup with warm bread but most of our happiness came from just being together. Tonight had been different. It was nice but a little sad. I thought of how much Papa and Rosie would have liked that hot chocolate. I missed our Papa's hugs.

I think Peter noticed I was down because he chose that moment to whisper, "Jurak, I hid the present in the suitcase. Get it; we can give it to her tonight."

I scrambled down and got the suitcase. Mama watched, curious. For a second, I was afraid it was gone, I couldn't see it nor feel it when I first opened the bottom. I breathed a huge sigh of relief when I found it, quickly closing my hand around it. I didn't want Mama to see just yet. I put the case away and stood up. Peter stood by me.

"We have a little gift for you, Mama. We want you to have a nice Christmas tomorrow." Peter was a bit solemn but I was taking this seriously as well. I reached my hand towards Mama. She held her hand, soft under mine, and waited. I dropped the small pin into it. She gasped.

"A beautiful angel! Dziękuję Ci, my sweet boys, thank you." A tear started in her eye.

Peter passed out the peppermint treats we had bought earlier and the three of us savored them together. Outside our window, the sky had turned pink and snow had started to fall. Mama wished us both a Happy Christmas and the three of us fell asleep.

The next day, Peter and I woke later than normal. Mama was already out, working in the kitchen, just like any day. As we dressed, Peter asked, "Jurak, what is that?" There was a sock, hanging on the post of the bed. It looked funny, all stretched and sagging. I had no idea what it was. Peter untied it and brought it to the bed.

"Jurak, look! Marbles and candy!" Peter was very excited. He poured the contents onto the bed so I could see too. There were four pieces of candy: two strawberry and two root beer, our favorites. There were marbles too.

"Presents!" Peter was as excited as anything. He pocketed half the treasure and told me to take the rest. We ran to the kitchen to show our mother.

We were too excited to watch where we were going and just at the bottom of the stairs was Mr. Joclav. I didn't drop my gaze, mimicking my older brother. We slowed down but didn't say anything, I could feel his stare on my back as we made our way, silent now, to the kitchen. As soon as we entered the kitchen, we forgot him.

Peter ran to our mother, showing her what we had found. I followed and showed her mine, the exact replica of what my brother already showed her. She laughed and pulled us close, kissing the tops of our heads. Miss Florence was smiling from across the kitchen.

Breakfast was good, the best we ever had. Mama called it "strudel." The warm pastry was sugary and soft and filled with hot apples. As usual, our milk washed it down filling up our normally empty stomachs. We were allowed to stay in the kitchen that day. The snow was so deep it had blocked the backdoor to the kitchen. Mama didn't hush us all day, and Miss Florence made us more hot chocolate. Peter and I played with our new marbles and talked with our mother all day. I noticed she wore her new pin on her shirt collar. I was very proud when she showed it to Miss Vicki.

We got an early lunch that day; there was the biggest bird I had ever seen, roasted brown. There were potatoes and bread. There was more pie and even more milk. Peter ate and ate. I think he ate all day. I had at least two helpings of everything. Afterwards, we laid out in front of the back entrance. Peter groaned and told me he ate too much. I had never known there was such a thing.

It must have been four o'clock when I remembered Rosa. Here it was Christmas, and I had forgotten her. Peter stole some of that roasted brown bird and we made our way to the front of our building. I hoped Rosa would be easy to find.

We were wearing our new coats and new shoes. My feet hurt before we even reached the door, but Mama had already given my old shoes to Miss Vicki so I resolved to just get used to the pain. The restaurant was busy as ever, and we waved to our mother. She was busy taking dishes to the back and just smiled at us, her arms full.

The street was busy, even with the cold and snow, and, at first, we couldn't find Rosa. We walked towards the back and called her name. I think she was sleeping somewhere warm because it sure took a while for her to come out. Peter took the bird from his pocket when she got there, and we sat on some overturned crates to feed her.

I was so happy to have her. She was soft when the world was hard. She was grateful when others were not. She was never selfish or demanding. She was a good friend. She liked the bird and licked our hands until there was no more taste on them. Then, she darted back to her own warm home. Peter and I kicked at the snow covering the door until we could open it and went back into the warm kitchen. It had been a good Christmas.

Another Loss

After that great Christmas, the world turned bitterly cold. It was so unbearable, Peter even stopped leaving the school at noon. We trudged to school in the cold, then trudged home in the cold, our heads bent low in the wind. January was a bleak month.

Peter and I were proud of how we looked in our new things. Our shoes were shiny and clean. Our coats were dark without frayed ends. There were no holes in our pockets. New clothes come with a downside though. My feet hurt, and I hated those shoes. They squeaked every time I took a step. My new coat was itchy, leaving my neck bright red. I never complained and especially not to Mama. That would have broken her heart.

She was so happy when she saw Peter and me after school in the fine things she had bought for us. Every time she saw us in our new things, she smiled broadly. Then, she would pat our heads as if we were very small children and tell us how good we looked. One day, I noticed Peter limping up to our room after dinner but he never complained either. We just hugged Mama and whispered our thanks.

I noticed that my teeth were no longer hurting and Peter stopped rubbing his cheek altogether. I thought it was because we stopped buying sweets, and Miss Kate no longer made our breakfast daily. Mama never did give us the extra sugar; she always warned it would rot our teeth. I didn't think too much more about my teeth or sugar since the pain had subsided. I forgot all about both until I noticed Peter's smile one day in mid-January.

My feet had finally worn my new shoes quiet and soft. My neck was still itching, but my arms were warm. Peter took his shoes off one night and grinned at me from across the room.

"My shoes are finally broken in, Jurak. They stopped hurting my feet!" He didn't sound surprised, just relieved. He must have worn in shoes before. Mine had always been hand-me-downs. I was contemplating that when I noticed a wide gap in his mouth.

His front tooth was gone. I went in for a closer look, "Peter, your tooth! It's gone!" I was horrified. If Peter lost his teeth, how could he eat?

"That is what happens to teeth, Jurak, don't you remember Papa's? He was missing a whole bunch! It means I am a man now." I was very impressed at this news. I didn't know Peter was a man. I thought he might be too short, but he *was* missing that tooth. He opened his mouth wide so I could look in. Peter was actually missing several teeth. I was awestruck. Here was my brother, a man.

We crawled into bed and were quiet. I was wondering what this change meant for our family. Men worked and moved from their families. *Would Peter move on?* I wondered. I didn't like that thought, so I pushed it far from my mind and tried to sleep. Peter didn't seem worried at all. I could hear his deep breathing almost at once.

A few weeks went by, and Peter stayed with us. I stopped worrying about him growing up and instead, focused on school. Miss Fink was a good teacher, and I was convinced she knew everything there was to know. She could spell, and read, and write, and add. She never made a mistake. I asked Miss Kate about her one day. I wanted to know how Miss Fink knew all she did.

"Well, some kids grow up and they nevah have to work. They have two parents and grandparents who all take care of 'em. They get to go to school and then they can teach children. I always had to work, my ma died when we were little and then our pa died. I nevah went to school. I lived with my sister 'til I heard about San Francisco. That's how I'm here. I'm on my way to San Francisco. I'm gunna live by the ocean," Miss Kate had a way that explained a lot without answering without answering my questions.

Peter and I kept going to school. I was very proud I could now read as well as Peter. Mama took the Sunday newspapers from the dining room each Sunday. All week, Peter and I would each read one article a night a loud. Mama would mend and listen, telling us over and over again how proud she was that we could read so well.

Thankfully, February was not as bleak as January, and March was even better. I was sure I felt the Earth turn back towards the sun. The days were longer. The wind still howled, but it didn't seem as cold. Peter even walked home without his hat on several occasions.

It was so nice, we resolved to start our trapping line again. We missed the pennies and the candy. That first Friday, we set off early, and I swear I heard Miss Fink breathed a sigh of relief. Peter had taken to asking all sorts of questions, often arguing how, what, and why as Miss Fink explained the answers. I didn't think she would miss us. We set our traps and walked back to town. It was still pretty chilly. We kept our hands stuffed deep into our pockets and bent our heads against the wind.

Smith's was full of shoppers, and Victoria didn't see us as we walked by. Rosa was following us, unhappy she had no fish for her efforts. She left us before we even entered the backdoor. Peter opened the door, and we were surprised to see Miss Vicki. I wanted to get right into the warmth, but Miss Vicki ushered us along saying she needed help with carrying something.

Peter and I had never helped her with carrying anything before, and I was sure I had never seen her do any amount of shopping. Peter told her we were cold and wanted to go inside. She stared us down for just a second or two, and of course, we relented. We had a soft spot for that lady, and she knew it.

She led us back into the chilly wind, down the main street, then all the way down to Smith's. She talked with Victoria and looked around until my stomach was really howling with hunger. Miss Vicki pretended not to notice and she ignored Peter's many pointed glares. After at least an hour, we finally left and walked right back to our building; she never bought a thing. It was strange. Rosa was at the backdoor when we got back. Miss Vicki pushed her way in front of us and entered the kitchen door first. I immediately followed right on her footsteps but found my way blocked.

Mr. Joclav stood in front of us, barring our entrance to the kitchen. Peter met his gaze, and I tried to be brave. He stretched his arms to either side of the doorframe, sneering down at us. Rosa stopped her purring. I was scared but didn't know what to do. I was getting colder standing there in the dark and I was so hungry. We didn't know what he wanted or why he was blocking us.

Moving slowly, Mr. Joclav reached down and grabbed Rosa by her tail. She howled in anger and fear. I tried but failed to reach her. Peter actually jumped at Mr. Joclav, stretching his hands upwards to my Rosa, but he was too short too.

"There's enough pussy in this building," we heard him mutter and he carried Rosa, still howling away from me. Mama heard the commotion and came running to the backdoor. I was too upset to explain, but Peter told her in clear detail. We could hear Rosa howling and Mama ran out to see what was happening. I heard a horrible sound right then; the sickening sound of bone smashing into brick, and Rosa immediately stopped yowling.

Mama stopped running and stood silently covering her mouth with her hands in shocked disbelief. We heard Mr. Joclav throw my Rosa's body over a fence. Then, he slowly lumbered his way back. He stopped in front of Mama and whispered, "You can keep them warm, but I own your happiness. As long as you work here, I own you." He eyed her up and down, slowly taking in each part of her body.

Mama ignored him and hurried back to us, ushering us through the door. She firmly shut it behind her, right on Mr. Joclav. We didn't stop in the kitchen. We just hurried up to our room where Mama shut the door and locked it. I spilled out onto the bed sobbing, already missing my dear friend. Peter swore.

"No! You will not talk like that, Peter. If you do, I will wash your mouth out. You will also leave Mr. Joclav alone. It is true he is vile and evil, but this room is all we have. Think: Where would we go? How would we eat?" Peter paced back and forth, glaring as Mama tried to comfort me.

A soft knock came to our door a few minutes later. It was Miss Kate with our dinner tray.

Mama helped me turn around, and Peter gave me my bowl of stew. I noticed Miss Kate gave us extra bread.

"Kat, we need you in the kitchen." Her voice was soft but Mama recognized it was not a request. She patted my knee and followed Miss Kate out.

In between sobs, I ate as much soup as I could and tried to swallow the bread. I tasted nothing. I hardly noticed my stomach filling up with food. Peter didn't speak. Rosa was gone, and there was nothing I could do, nothing Mama could do, nothing Peter could do.

The next few days are a blur in my memory. The weather grew cold again as a late storm blew through. It seemed appropriate—my heart felt so cold, the weather may as well as match it. Monday morning, Peter and I walked to school. Friday, we checked our traps. We even went to our fishing hole and fished. My heart just wasn't into it, and I missed Rosa.

Nils

The days grew longer and even though I missed Rosa, I was doing good.

Miss Fink told me she was proud of my hard work and sent good news home to Mama. I would pass into the next grade. Peter would as well. Mama was very proud and told anyone who would listen.

Peter expanded our trapping line. We still trapped rabbits, but he wanted to start targeting fox and whatever else may come our way. He had a good plan. Instead of setting only one trap in each little area, we would set two. We extended our line from the fields all the way to the creek. He figured if we did this, we could make up to twenty cents a week just from trapping. Peter also found another buyer so we wouldn't need to rely on that old woman anymore. He said he had plans for our money; we would buy new traps every week until we had enough to fill our line.

Peter was a perfectionist with those traps. He laid them each night and checked them every afternoon before we fished or swam. He taught me to never let animal suffer and how to skin and clean them. It was alright work. I liked it better than sitting inside at school. We hid our coins in the bottom of our suitcase without telling Mama. She would figure it out soon enough.

One day, I woke up discovering I had lost a tooth. I wasn't ready for this. I couldn't be a grown up and I wasn't ready to leave Mama. I was so embarrassed, I refused to talk or even open my mouth much. It took two days for Mama to drag the truth from me. Finally, in a flood of tears, I explained my fears of my impending adulthood. We were doing our wash and I had just climbed out of the tub. Mama pulled me close, ignoring my wet hair in her chest. I could feel her shoulders shake and she didn't speak. When she let me go, I saw her wipe tears out of her eyes but she told me I would be alright; I didn't have to go just yet. I thought she had cried with me until I heard her telling Miss Vicki about it later. The tears were from laughter, nothing else. I wasn't a man yet and from the way Miss Vicki and Mama were laughing, I had a long way to go. I was more relieved than offended.

Life went along alright for the three of us. It wasn't glamorous, but we were together each night. Mama told us that is what counted most. Peter and I noticed her smiling more as the days went on, and it was nice to hear her laugh. Mama was doing good and it showed.

She walked down the hallways with a graceful strength admired by all. She didn't look away from Mr. Joclav when he looked her over. She laughed with Miss Vicki and Miss Kate and kept up on all her duties. She started going to mass every Sundays. Her eyes showed a resilient healing each time she woke. She was no longer tired and ill with a stretched mouth. I was so proud of her even though I wished she wouldn't make us go to church.

Peter hated it more than I. We sat, we kneeled, we prayed, and most of all, we fidgeted. I think Mama liked the rest; after all, she stood and ran all week. For Peter and me, it was a nightmare trying to be still. Every few minutes, she pinched us hard under our arms to make us quiet down again. As much as those little pinches hurt, we sure forgot quickly. We would be back to fidgeting only to earn them again.

One Saturday evening, I noticed a man we had seen a few times before. He was in our restaurant, and I could tell he was watching for our mama. I knew he watched for her whenever he was in. He never said much to her. He just took his food and quietly ate. He was young and very quiet.

Most young men had something to prove—they would shout and run to get attention. This man was different though. He always ate quickly and paid before he left. He didn't try and grab anyone. He always took his hat off when he came in our building.

Mama didn't seem to take any special notice of him. She was busy, I suppose. The man ate and quietly left. The very next day, I saw him in church. I had never seen him there before, and he looked absolutely lost.

He didn't know when to kneel or when to pray. He tried being respectful but he was a mess. I guessed he wasn't Catholic. I saw his eyes wander over to us, catching every pinch and fidget as we kneeled and sang our way through the service. After the priest dismissed us, he came right over to our Mama.

Hat in hand, he looked as fidgety as Peter and I were. Peter glared at him.

"Hello there," came a quiet, soothing voice that caught Mama's attention.

She looked over. "Hallo." Then she turned to us and said, "Boys, come."

I was so happy church was over and we could leave, I raced on out the door, leaving Mama with the quiet young man. I glanced back and saw him gesture her ahead of him down the aisle. Mama smiled, very pleased.

We walked back to our building, and Mama and the man followed. They didn't talk. They just walked along watching us. I noticed the young man looked pleased and when we got to the backdoor of the kitchen, he asked, "Could I come talk to you again, Katarzyna?" So, they had introduced themselves. I raised my eyebrows to Peter. We paid closer attention. Our beautiful Mama, always graceful and perfect, looked flustered. I hadn't seen her look like that before.

Color rose into her cheeks and her eyes widened. She didn't say any words back at all; she just nodded and smiled. Then, she ushered us inside and followed quickly.

Peter and I weren't going to waste such a day indoors, we ran out almost as soon as the door closed behind us. Mama was busy, and we wanted to check our trapline. The quiet man was just turning the corner as we ran past him. Peter and I didn't notice him follow us.

I followed Peter out to the end of town into the open fields towards the creek. Our first trap on the line had trapped a fox just two days before. I could tell Peter was hoping for another. The trap was hidden well, right down in a little hollow near a tree not too far from the creek. There were actually two, just as Peter planned, and we knew we had something—we could hear it before we saw it.

Peter skidded to a stop and peered over the edge and sure enough, one trap was full. A good-sized fox was yowling trying to escape. Peter clubbed him to sleep, and we set about collecting the pelt.

"You boys seem to know what you're doing." The voice came from nowhere, and Peter dropped the fox in his surprise. The quiet man followed us to our line, and I could tell Peter didn't like that. I myself wasn't too sure how I felt about it either.

"Don't worry, I won't take your catch. I just was curious where you were running to in such a hurry." His voice was soft and soothing, curious and honest. Before long, Peter and I were telling him all about our line. We told how we started with just the two traps and grown it into twelve. The man was impressed; he raised his eyebrows, "How did you know where to put the traps?"

I couldn't answer, I never did figure out how Peter know just where to lay them. Peter just shrugged and muttered, "It just feels right."

He followed us up our line where we collected four more pelts. We finally reached the creek. Peter and I splashed around, washing off the blood and hair from skinning our catch. It was warm, and I was wondering if we could swim when Peter asked, "Why are you following our Mama to church? You don't act Catholic." If Mama had been there, she would have admonished his rudeness. I didn't care. I was curious, so I waited in silence.

"It just feels right."

Peter and I looked up, and Peter laughed. "My name's Peter, and this is Jurak."

"Mine is Nils." I thought the name fitted him as he was quiet and unassuming. "I came here from Sweden. I got this job working the railroad and now I am thinking I will live here. People are nice, and I have work."

Peter looked over at me, his eyes thoughtful. It looked like Nils was going to stay. After that day, we saw Nils quite often. He went to church but still didn't understand about the kneeling. We saw him eating in the restaurant. He ate there most nights and every Sunday. He never bothered Mama. He seemed content to wait and just enjoyed being near her. I could tell that it both pleased her and made her nervous.

Nils also followed us out to our trapline every Saturday. He never pushed in to show us the right way to do things, he let us to figure it out. He watched and listened as we told him about school. I told him about Victoria. That made him laugh and Peter grumble. I told him about our sweets and how Peter bought us one each week and that my favorite was strawberry. Nils said he liked ginger. It was the only thing I found I didn't really like about him.

A few weeks later, I told him about Rosa. Peter was swimming and being loud, but I was missing Rosa. I was just sitting on the edge of the bank. Somehow, I thought she would have liked where it was warm and sunny. Nils asked me how I was, and I got tearful. I told him what a good cat and friend she had been. I told him how she liked her fish and how she always followed me without me having to ask. I told him how she had watched over Mama. His brow furrowed the more I talked. I finally told him how Mr. Joclav smashed her to death. It broke my heart even after so many weeks.

"Rosa never hurt anyone. She never went inside and she never took food from the kitchen. I don't know why he killed her," I finished.

Nils didn't say anything. He was quiet and looked out over the water, watching Peter for a time. I caught my breath and controlled my sobs while he watched.

"Some people are just mean, Jurak. They take anything soft and nice and try to ruin it. Life is hard, but no one should be that hard." He ruffled my hair. I felt better, but Nils looked distant the rest of the day.

The next day was Sunday and we went to church. Nils now sat with us which was nice because Mama forgot to pinch us for fidgeting. She was kept too busy whispering to him to kneel or stand. Afterwards, he walked us home. Sundays were nice.

Falls

Nils came around more and more often. Peter finally asked Mama about it one Monday after our washing. "Mama, what does Nils want with us?"

Mama was busy with her back turned, but I could tell she was smiling. The sides of her face had grown full. She took her time answering. "He is a nice man, Peter. I am happy to call him a friend."

Peter and I glanced at each other. We now had even less information than before Peter asked. Mama finished with her hair, and Peter and I helped carry our things back to our room. We hung our wash and Mama opened our window further. Summer was wonderful. Days weren't too hot and each evening there was a soft breeze cooling the earth around us. The noise from the street mingled with the noise of our building. As rough as life had been and in spite of our losses, the three of us had somehow made a fine home.

"I like Nils very much," Mama whispered as we were falling asleep. I smiled. I liked him too.

A few days went by and Mama started talking about school again. Peter and I had an excellent trapping business going. We fished every day and feasted every night. I didn't want to think about sitting in school all day. I certainly didn't want to think about the cold that would envelop the world again. Summer was too good. I heard Peter sigh deeply. He hated the thought of winter too.

One day, on our way to check our trapping line, we ran into Miss Fink. Peter and I both liked her a lot, but the chance encounter put a damper on our day. She smiled at us and we straightened our backs to offer our hellos. She asked, "What have you been up to this summer?" Peter told her all about our line, and I told her about fishing. She smiled and nodded. We didn't think to ask how her summer was.

"I don't want to start school again, Jurak," Peter said as she walked away. He didn't need an answer. He was just stating what every kid feels like at the end of every summer. Peter and I were totally free and giving that up came at a great price, especially for Peter.

He hated the feel of long sleeves. He hated the lack of wind in his face. He hated someone else being in charge of his minutes and hours. School, for him, was little more than a detention reminding us of the summer we lost each year.

I was content, though, but all of August still stretched in front of us. I tried to forget the upcoming school year and enjoyed all our adventures. Each morning, bright and early, Mama or Miss Florence would give us a good helping of bread and milk. Then, we ran to the edge of town. Before we took off through the fields, I would stand and breathe in all the good smells of the countryside. Peter and I ran up and down our trapping line and spent our afternoons in the water. Even though we spent each day the same, we never tired of the routine. I think the fresh air brought something new to us each and every day.

Nils loyally followed us every Saturday. One of those afternoons, he asked us about our father. He wanted to know what he was like. Peter asked him why he wanted to know about him.

"I want to know you better, that is all," Nils said softly.

"Ok, well do you know about our Rosie?" Peter challenged him. I couldn't understand why Peter was so defensive. Nils had only asked about our father. He had never met him and, in this life, he never would. It didn't seem like something to be defensive over. Nils was a nice man. Nils shook his head. He didn't know about our Rosie.

I gave a sad smile. My heart ached for Rosie and our Papa still, but we didn't talk about either of them often enough.

"She was our ugly baby. She looked like a potato," I explained.

"She wasn't ugly and she wasn't a potato," Peter sounded almost angry. "She was our baby sister. You can ask Mama; she was perfect. She had golden curls and pink cheeks. She was soft just like Mama. She died after Christmas two years ago after she got a cough."

"Well, before she got the curls, she looked like a potato," I explained to Nils. "After she grew up, she was pretty with pink cheeks. She always smiled at us, and we had to hold her a lot while Mama cleaned up our house or made us dinner. We were helping her learn to walk when she got sick."

Nils looked thoughtful. "I had a baby sister. Everyone told us she was beautiful, but now that you mention it, she did look a little like a potato when she was first born." I shot a triumphant look at Peter. After all, it wasn't Rosie's fault she had looked like a potato. We loved her even when she looked like one. "She died of a cough, just like your Rosie, when she was very small. Our mother cried for days and didn't like leaving her in the ground in the cold. I didn't like it. It seemed lonesome. I had a grandmother who was kind though. She told us the angels would keep her company, and I believe her. I don't think your Rosie or our little potato are alone. You see, potatoes grow in bunches after all."

Peter watched Nils with a softer expression. "Well, Rosie didn't look much like a potato if you ask me, but it is nice to think she isn't alone." Peter sounded very old. "Our mama was terribly sad for days after she died, just like yours. It seemed like only a few days went by and then our Papa got sick too. Then, he just died," Peter's voice caught, and I saw him wipe a tear away. "He just died, and there was nothing Jurak and I could do. We wanted to work to help Mama, but we are just kids. Then, she left. She left him with us in our house for hours. His eyes were open and his body was dead." Peter had to stop talking.

"Our Aunt Anya—she's Mama's sister—finally came and helped us. She tried to close his eyes, but only one wanted to shut. We left him and went to stay with her. We never saw him after that. He was big and tall. He was loud. He made all of us believe him no matter what he said. He told us stories about dragons in the mines and old women hunting children in the mountains." I had never talked to anyone, not even Peter or Mama about Papa since we left our house. "He worked all the time for us, and Mama was very proud. She told us he would do anything for us, even steal if he had to. I thought he would live forever."

The three of us were very quiet for a long time after that. Nils patted Peter's back and rubbed my shoulder when we left. None of us ever said anything more about that day, but we were closer after that, and Peter never got defensive with Nils again. Not ever.

We didn't see Nils in church that Sunday and we could tell Mama was disappointed. I watched her look for him. Her eyes scanned the church over and over again. She pinched more than ever that day and after the service, she hurried home, snapping at us to hurry. I wasn't used to such a mood from Mama on a Sunday, and my stomach had that pinched feeling. "Where is Nils?" Peter whispered to me. I just shook my head; I had no idea.

We didn't see Nils the rest of that day nor all the way into next week. He finally showed up the next Saturday. Peter asked where he had been. Nils told us he had business. We accepted that answer, but I told him how much Mama had missed him. I think he liked that because he smiled a big smile.

We did our trapping and fishing and brought it all back to town. When Mama saw Nils waiting at the backdoor with us, she acted as if she hadn't missed him. She barely looked at him as she told us, "You boys come in and wash up. I will fry this fish." Then, she acted like she had only just noticed Nils was with us. "Oh hello, Nils. Are you staying for fish?"

Nils ate with us sometimes but not often. I hoped he would stay, but Mama didn't sound too welcoming. Nils smiled big, and Peter and I kept quiet. He nodded to Mama. Mama didn't even smile back. Peter and I pushed in—we were hungry.

Nils took Mama's hand before she went in. "I will be in church tomorrow. I was sorry to miss it last week," Mama smiled. After that, she was nicer.

School started the next week, and Peter and I were penned indoors for at least half each day. Miss Fink said she was happy to have us all back but she glanced out the windows as often as everyone else. Then, she dismissed us five minutes early all week. No one complained.

Life took on a new normal in the following weeks, and Peter and I kept up our trapping line pretty good, even with having to do school in the mornings. The days were getting colder and one day, we woke to frost.

That day was a turning point for the three of us, though, it would take looking back and remembering it all to know life turned that day.

It was a normal morning. Peter and I ate our bread and milk and then ran to school. The frost didn't stay long. Miss Fink had gotten used to having students again and did not dismiss us early. I followed Peter out of town to check our traps. A terrible yowling noise greeted us.

The line was large even with two people working it. During the summer, no animal had to wait long because Peter and I checked the traps in the mornings and afternoons. Thanks to the nuisance of school, we now only had the afternoons to check the traps. It was awful. It sounded as if some animal had been there all night. I didn't like the sound. It was angry, hostile at its own stupidity for getting caught. It was scared. Animals weren't stupid—it knew its life was over. Above all that, it was in pain. Peter looked unnerved, but we headed towards the noise anyways. Peter grabbed a heavy stick.

There, in our first trap was a small fox. It was beautiful. Its red hair glinted in the sunlight, and the black tipped ears shone. Its right rear foot was caught and mangled. Judging by its sluggish movements, it had struggled through the night and morning. The fox would lie down, panting, breathing deep for air, and closed its eyes. While he was laying there, it looked as if he was trying to forget he was trapped. Then, he would catch his breath and leap far into the air, shaking its foot madly, trying to free itself from the trap. Next, he bit his own leg, all the while making the most horrible noise. Peter and I had trapped for nearly two years. We were used to the noises and death brought to those animals, but this one unnerved us.

We didn't watch long. Peter ran down to it and clubbed it twice. I was so grateful the horrible noise stopped. I believe the fox was grateful as well—it never even fought back. The rest of the lines were empty.

The fox left us a beautiful little pelt. That old woman paid double the normal price. I could tell Peter was glad for that. As we made our way home, I noticed the sun was already gone, and the evening was cold. I wished we had our coats. Peter was rubbing his arms too. Winter was nearly here.

Our building was cold that night. The radiators hadn't been turned on, and I was glad we slept over the kitchen. It would be warmer that way. Mama was in a hurry that night. She was distracted by something she didn't want to share with us. She tried to smile her way through dinner and asked us about school and Miss Fink. That pinching feeling in my stomach was there, and she didn't eat much. I could tell Peter noticed too.

Mr. Joclav was in our hallway. We didn't see him until after we had climbed the stairs. Peter glared at him, but I lowered my eyes. I couldn't remember the last time we even saw him. I had almost forgotten the greasy hair, stained teeth, and his grizzled chin. Mama put us behind her and, though her step slowed, she led us towards our room, key at the ready.

Mr. Joclav blocked the entire hallway. Mama made herself as small as possible, edging by him, but he leaned in. It made hair on the back of my neck stand straight up. Peter's hands were in fists.

"It's getting cold out, Kat. Supposed to be the coldest winter in a decade; is that worth anything this year?" His voice was soft, daring, and threatening. I could tell Mama didn't like him so close. She didn't answer, and he roughly grabbed her left arm, pulling her close to him. He looked her up and down, "That room was good for one year. The next payment is almost due."

Releasing her, he grinned down at Peter and me, then sauntered off down the hall. Mama was shaking so much she dropped the key. I picked it up and unlocked our door. None of us spoke. We readied for bed and climbed in. It was warm with all three of us there, but Mama shook for a long time that night.

I tried to forget about Mr. Joclav in the hallway and so did Peter and Mama. Maybe he was wrong and winter wouldn't be so bad this year. Maybe we wouldn't even need heat in our room.

Nils noticed Mama was worried at church that Sunday, though. I heard him ask her about it, and she finally told him she was worried for the cold. She told him the cold scared her. He just nodded. When we got back to our building, Mr. Joclav was in the kitchen door.

"Well howdy, stranger," he said too loudly to Nils. "Now, why are you hanging around out back here when we have a nice place up front?" It wasn't a question, and Nils didn't answer. "I see you know our Kat. You know, she been workin' here, what is it, Kat? Nearly two years? One of my best girls." I saw my mother looked to the ground, ashamed. "At least, that's what I think. Of course, she has a debt to pay. It comes due every year around this time, so I don't know if she will be around much longer. It's worth it though, ain't it, Kitty? It gets cold and people get sick. They die. Best to pay your debt early; keep everyone safe that way." I had never heard anyone call our mother Kitty. I didn't like the way he said it.

Nor, it seemed, did Nils and Peter. They both stood, glaring at Mr. Joclav and Mama stood, shoulders and head down. I thought I saw a tear on her cheek. Nils noticed too. His look changed from anger to understanding. He saw my mother there with her two boys, raw red hands, and head bent in shame. If he was looking at Mr. Joclav with distaste before, he was looking at him with absolute hate now. Nils put his hat back on and never dropped his gaze from Mr. Joclav. Mr. Joclav put a heavy arm around Mama's thin shoulders.

I thought Nils would lose all control, but he stood his ground. He told Mr. Joclav to remove his arm. I never understood why, but Mr. Joclav removed his arm. Then, he went inside without another word.

"Katarzyna, I am here for you," Nils whispered, but Peter and I could still hear. He didn't wrap his arms around our mother, he only lifted her chin so she looked into her eyes. "You are not of this place; you are not that man's." He left us then. Mama's eyes closed briefly and she ushered us inside. Thankfully, Mr. Joclav was nowhere to be seen.

Miss Kate and Miss Vicki were there to help. They made Mama sit and brought her something warm to drink. Her shoulders were shaking again. Miss Kate asked us about our traps, but I overheard Miss Vicki talking to Mama.

"Kat, you will have to pay, we all do. It's too cold to survive anywhere else, and how can you save any money with two children to look for? You can't leave. It won't be as bad as last year. We can plan this time. I can slip something into his drink, calm him down. You can do this," Miss Vicki held Mama's white hands. She got up and walked around the back of Mama and held her shoulders. Mama sat there and cried. She didn't even try to hide it. Miss Kate stopped talking and the three of us watched Miss Vicki hold Mama, trying to keep her shoulders from shaking.

Mama tried to talk in between sobs and it was hard to understand her. In between her Polish and hiccups, I understood enough. She missed our Papa, she missed our Rosie, and she missed being our mother. Miss Kate got up first, but Peter and I were right behind her. The four of us held onto her, letting her cry it out until she was done. She drew a deep, rasping breath in and told Miss Vicki she was tired. I saw Mr. Joclav peer in with a satisfied grin on his ugly mouth.

Miss Vicki told Miss Kate to help Mama up to our room and she told us boys to go on outside. "I will take care of her today; you go and do whatever you do in the afternoons. We will watch over her." We trusted her, so we left. Ominously, we didn't catch anything that day.

Nils was sitting in the restaurant when Peter and I walked back. He and Mr. Joclav were glaring at each other from across the place. Nils food was in front of him, untouched. Judging from the look on Nils' face, I wasn't too sure he was aware his food was in front of him. We didn't hang around there.

Miss Kate brought Peter and I our dinner, "They been out there awhile, lookin' at each other like that. Nils never said nothing to Mr. Joclav. Mr. Joclav never said nothing to Nils. I don't know what's gunna happen." Peter raised his eyebrows at me.

Miss Vicki told us to go upstairs as soon as our tray was empty even though we had taken our time with eating that night. We made our way slowly through the kitchen ignoring Miss Vicki's orders to hurry up. Nils was still out there and so was Mr. Jocalv. As soon we were out of the kitchen, we ran up the stairs. Mama was already asleep. Peter and I were careful not to wake her. Our building was louder than ever that night.

The next Sunday, Nils was waiting for us outside the church. I thought Mama looked extra special that day. She had taken the time to braid her hair and her eyes were bright. Nils was standing there, hat in hands, watching, patient as ever. He didn't turn towards the church as normal but led us off towards the city park. Peter looked surprised when Mama didn't complain.

It was a nice autumn day. There was hardly any wind and it was warm. The trees were turning and the town was quiet. Normally, Peter and I would run on ahead, but today we followed Nils and Mama. They took their time talking so quietly that Peter and I couldn't hear. We ended up beneath a large tree near the creek. Peter and I ran to the water, tossing in stones and small sticks, ignoring Mama and Nils. Finally, bored with our little water games, we turned back towards them.

Nils was kissing Mama.

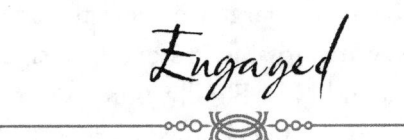

Engaged

Mama and Nils were engaged, Mama explained one day a few weeks after the park day. "Engaged means Nils and I will marry, and the four of us will be a family." I didn't know what to think of that. I thought Nils was very nice and Peter liked him, too. I had a few doubts, though. We were the leftovers from our family. I wasn't too sure how to fit Nils in and as much as Peter said he liked Nils, I could tell he wasn't sure either. Was Nils our new papa?

Peter didn't ask any questions, and I wasn't ready to ask mine. We just gave Mama a hug and climbed into bed. As I rolled over, I stared at the wall thinking a long time.

Ever since the terrible day when we left Rosie in the cold ground, life had been different. Everything changed. Papa died and we had to leave our house. I didn't think our home now was so bad. After all, we saw Mama every day and there was enough food. Our room was small but warm. *What could Nils offer to make our life better?*

I wasn't sure Nils could make our lives better. Peter and I were doing good in school and with our trapping. I didn't want to give up fishing in the afternoons. I liked our freedom. I wasn't sure I wanted to give up all that. If Mama married Nils, where would he sleep? Our room was too small for another person. Those questions kept me awake a long time that night, and I didn't hear Mama or Peter sleeping much either.

Miss Kate asked Peter and me about Nils a few days later as she got us our dinner tray. Normally, Peter and I took the tray. After a little while, we were joined by Miss Vicki or Miss Kate or Mama. We normally ate our dinners in a small crook, just off the kitchen. There were three steps down making it perfect for balancing the tray on our knee while we sat on a short step eating. Miss Kate sat on the step above us watching.

"So, ya like him?" As usual, Miss Kate was very direct.

I nodded. I really did like Nils. Peter nodded too.

"That's good. Course, I never knew your papa but I never seen Kat smile like this either." Miss Kate made a good point there. I hadn't seen Mama this happy in a long time either. Her shoulders weren't sagging all the time and the dark circles under her eyes were not quite so dark. "Nils is a good guy to take you two in, that's for sure." Miss Kate rubbed my shoulder, got up, and walked away.

"You know, she's right," Peter told me. "Think about it. Nils isn't as old as Mama; he doesn't have any kids. He's awfully nice to us. I don't think he's the sort of guy that hits or yells too much either. Not like some men who help women." Peter's voice grew dark. I knew he was talking about Mr. Joclav.

I knew Peter *was* right. Nils was a good person. We never heard him yell, and I don't think he was one to hit. He always talked softly and held his hat in hand.

"What will happen, though? Where will we live? Will Nils live with us?" I asked.

Peter shook his head. "I'm not sure; we never saw where he lives."

Peter and I only knew a few things about Nils. He worked for the railroad and he must have been really strong because his arms and hands were huge. He laid railroad ties. Miss Vicki told us it was a good job, and Miss Kate said he was rich. Mama told us the truth.

"Nils came to this country just the same as your Papa and I. He was looking for a new life, for something better. He got here and he found out how tough it is to make a new life, just like your Papa and I found. But Nils, he didn't want to mine, so he found a job working for the railroad. It is a good job, with clean air and not as dangerous as mining. It is hard work, though. They pay well and have a savings system. It will let Nils save for later in life, when he doesn't want to work anymore. Nils is not rich but Nils does well for this life." Mama wasn't boasting but she looked pleased.

I think Mama worried it was too good to be true. Small things bothered her like never before. Our room was always clean but now it was immaculate. She wanted the bed made perfectly. It was to be kept very straight. She wanted the curtain pulled back just right. We were shushed so often we nearly forgot how to talk. We weren't allowed to talk about Nils anywhere but outside the building or in our room. Miss Kate and Miss Vicki stopped asking us so many questions. They just winked and smiled at us a lot. That part was fun. It was like we all shared a big secret.

Peter and I went to school. We never told anyone about Nils. We were too busy to talk much anyways. Our trapping line was busier than ever and the fishing was good each day. We were too busy to talk about it all. The next Saturday, Nils followed us out to our fishing hole.

Nils sat opposite us and chewed on a blade of grass for some time. Finally, he said, "I asked your mama to marry me. The first time I saw her, I was riding the trolley car. I had just moved to town. She was standing on the sidewalk. She was so beautiful; I had never seen anyone like her before. I couldn't forget her. I felt like I had to know her. I found out her name and then I found out she has two boys. I know your Papa was a good man and I am sorry you lost him."

Peter and I watched Nils, wondering what he was going to say next. Surely, he knew Mama told us they were getting married.

"I can't marry your mama without asking you boys first. I need to know you boys are all right with the idea. I love her and I want to marry her, but she was your mama first." I liked how Nils always treated us like we were his equals. "So, is it alright with you boys if I marry her?"

I looked at Nils closely. He was a tall man. He had brown hair and kind, brown eyes. I felt good about him being married to our mama but I had a few questions. "Well, Nils, I think it's fine you marry Mama. I just don't know where you're gonna sleep. Our bed's awful crowded and our room is so tiny. There's hardly room for us."

Nils could have laughed at my simple question. Instead, he looked into my eyes and then into Peter's. "Well, I'm afraid if we get married, you boys will have to move again. Your mama told me about your room and how small it is. You're right, I don't think another person will fit. If you come with me, I want to show you something."

Nils stood up and put his hat on and started off towards town. Peter and I scrambled to collect our things. We had to run to catch up with him. Nils walked right onto the main street, then continued up towards the part of town Peter and I tried to stay away from.

This part of town boasted new houses. Each house was a neat square with a large window and chimney. Neat square yards accompanied each. The houses were all the same but some were white and some were yellow. None of the houses were connected, and there were no big buildings like ours on this street. Peter and I knew some boys from this part of town. They were nice. Nils walked almost to the end of the street. I wondered what we were doing here.

He stopped in front of a white squared house with blue trim. He waited for us and pointed, "This is where I thought we'd live. I bought it a few weeks ago and have been putting furniture in it." Nils watched us as we looked over the house. "I haven't shown your mama yet; it's supposed to be a surprise. I wanted to surprise all of you, but you boys deserve to know where your new home will be."

I didn't know what to say; Peter kept quiet too. Nils walked around to the back of the house and opened a door. "Here is the kitchen. And if you boys come inside, I can show you the rest."

Our house had its own kitchen, its own bathroom, complete with running water. There were two bedrooms. It had a living room with a couch and two chairs. The kitchen had a table and four chairs. One bedroom had one big bed and the other held two smaller beds. *What would Mama do with all those rooms*, I wondered. Peter asked who else would be living with us.

Nils smiled, "Well, for now, this house is just for us four. I suppose if anyone else comes along or needs a place to stay, we can decide then." Nils beckoned us out and locked the door. We followed Nils back to our building.

On our way, I asked him when he would marry our mama. He said they hadn't set a date but he wanted to as soon as possible.

As we walked up to our building, I noticed it was much more gray than white. When we went inside, I realized how dirty the kitchen was.

"I sure hope they get a move on things," Peter whispered as we waited for Mama to fry up our fish. "That place looks nice, and I think Mama will like the blue paint." I was too afraid to talk out loud much—I didn't want to give away the surprise.

Somehow, I kept my mouth shut all the next week. Mama asked why I was so quiet and even worried I was sick, but I kept my word. I never told. On Friday morning, she told us to come right home after school. "And boys, I mean *right* after you leave school. We have plans this afternoon," Mama grinned at us.

Peter and I ran off laughing—we never knew Mama knew we cut class every day.

We left the schoolyard right at noon and ran all the way back to our building. We were very excited—we never had plans before. Miss Vicki met us at the kitchen door.

She whispered, "I am looking after you for a bit. Your mama is already gone. You boys come inside but be quiet." Miss Vicki was acting strange, we lived here after all. She didn't have to sneak us in or look after us. We could just go to our room if Mama wasn't here. She hurried us up the stairs, towards the washroom. "Your things are already in there, you two be quick and wash up. Put your clean clothes on."

Peter and I looked at each other; we couldn't even argue, we were so surprised. It was Friday, not Monday, and we had never bathed in the middle of any day. I followed Peter in and we shut the door without questioning the order.

"You boys are filthy; wash twice!" came another whispered order from Miss Vicki. I washed and rewashed. Peter looked me over and pointed me back to the tub. I grumbled and had to wash again too.

Peter looked at my nails and inspected the area behind my ears. I washed his back and after what seemed like hours of washing, we were finally done. My skin was pink from all the scrubbing and our hair squeaked when Miss Vicki pulled a comb through. "Your hair, it is too curly to be wasted on boys. You don't ever care." She was right; I didn't care, and those curls hurt when she combed.

We pulled on our clean clothes and followed her out. She put a finger to her mouth and carefully, quietly, led the way down the long hallway. She didn't bring us to our room nor did we follow her down to the kitchen again. Instead, she took us to the end of the hall to the door that opened to the fire escape.

"You boys, you go straight down these stairs and then meet me outside in front of the building. You wait for me if I am not there. Take care not to get dirty or tear your shirts or pants." Then, she handed us our dirty clothes and towels she had neatly bundled together and pointed us out the door. Peter and I obeyed her orders.

We hardly ever got to go down that fire escape. It was another exciting adventure. The metal stairs were open and shaky. I grew dizzy as we spiraled closer to the ground. Miss Vicki wasn't there yet. We waited, just as she'd told us to. We waited a long time.

After what I thought were hours, I peeked around the side. Mama wasn't out front and neither was Miss Vicki. I could tell Peter was getting as nervous as I was while we waited. I wondered why we were in clean clothes and why we had to bathe. The street was normal. There were the typical people out, with the typical noise.

After a while longer, Miss Vicki walked up behind us, startling Peter. Miss Kate was with her. They had put on nice dresses and neither of them wore aprons. Miss Kate looked absolutely delighted as she and Miss Vicki led us up the street. Peter shoved our bundle to me and ran ahead. Those women led us to a big, important looking building right in the middle of town. The sign labeled it as *Town Hall.* I saw Nils inside. Someone made him clean up too, I could tell.

His hair was neatly combed. His pants were clean and his shirt was all tucked in. Even his boots looked clean. He smiled at us and nodded to Miss Vicki and Miss Kate. "She's in there," he said, pointing off to our right.

Miss Vicki brought us in to a large room, opposite to where Nils pointed. They sat us down in a row of chairs, near the front. She followed Miss Kate out the door across the hall. They knocked on the door and hurried through it.

I looked all around. That pinching feeling was back in my stomach. Peter and I still had not been told what was going on, and I was still holding our bundle. Nils came over and took the bundle. He put it down at the back of the room. It was only then I noticed how happy he looked. "Today is the day, boys. Today is when I marry your mama."

"Well, that explains a lot," I told him. "Miss Vicki made us wash *twice*." Peter nodded vigorously. Nils smiled and asked us to be patient for just a little while longer.

I was terribly excited. We only had to wait a few more minutes. Miss Vick and Miss Kate came in first and sat just behind us. Then, a door opened in the back. There was our mama. Her hair was all up tucked into a new hat. Her dress was new, too. It was the prettiest dress we ever saw here wear. It fell just below her knees and had lace for the sleeves. She was carrying some white flowers that I knew would make me sneeze if I got too close. Her eyes looked happy when she saw us sitting there. Miss Vicki told us to stand and put our shoulders straight.

Nils waited quietly for Mama to join him up at the front. I hadn't noticed before, but now I saw another man there. He had a loud, kind voice. He asked Mama if she wanted to marry Nils. She nodded. Then, he asked Nils if he wanted to marry Mama. Nils grinned his response. I heard a sniffle and turned to see Miss Vicki take out a handkerchief. She wiped at her cheeks. That was all that happened. It only took a few minutes.

The man told us they were married now. Nils kissed Mama so exuberantly, I wasn't sure how her hat stayed on. Then, he led her out the door. I remembered our bundle as the four of us followed them out the door.

When we got outside, Nils kissed Mama again and said, "I have a reservation at the hotel for lunch today. Miss Vicki and Miss Kate, I hope you come too." Mama kissed Nils cheek.

She looked into my eyes. "I am very happy for us; I will tell you why we kept it so quiet later." She kissed Peter's cheek and took my hand in both of hers. "We aren't going back to our room; Nils has a surprise for us after lunch." Peter and I grinned at each other. She hadn't seen the house yet.

That was the best lunch of our life. It was in the best hotel in town. It was on the good end of town. All the tables had tablecloths and Mama made us put the napkins in the front of our shirts before lunch arrived. Nils got her a bubbly drink that was pink. Miss Vicki was "terribly impressed" with everything. Mama and Nils ordered our food for us and while we waited, we watched our mama.

She looked like a different woman. Her eyes were happy and her hair shiny. She smiled, showing her whole mouth instead of hiding her stained teeth. Mama was always graceful and today she shined more than ever. I noticed how careful Nils was with her. He was as gentle with her as if he was touching the most delicate flower. He sat very close to her and hardly looked anywhere else the whole day.

We ate our fill and laughed a lot. When all the food was gone, Nils led us out. The three ladies hugged.

Peter and I hugged them. When we parted ways, I saw Miss Kate brush tears from her eyes. They walked north, and we turned south.

Nils led us all the way down to the neat street we visited before. Peter picked up the bundle when I dropped it. Mama was very quiet. I noticed her grip on Nils arm tighten as we neared the little white square trimmed in blue.

Nils was so excited, he picked her up. "Boys, get the door!" He carried her right over the threshold. Mama's arms were wrapped around his neck, and he gently placed her on the ground in her new living room. She was shaking. Peter and I just stood, not sure what to do. Peter held onto the bundle.

Mama was crying and laughing and asking Nils what this was. He took her by the hand and led her around. He showed her the kitchen and living room and all of it. Mama couldn't talk. She was still shaking and by now she was really crying. I heard her whisper that she loved him.

As the evening grew cooler, Nils showed Mama how to warm up our house and how to work the lights. Peter and I sat at the table in the kitchen as the sky grew dark, playing with the deck of cards Peter always kept with him.

The neat little square warmed quickly. Nils and Mama sat talking in the living room late into the night. Finally, Mama reached up and unpinned her hat. "Thank you, Nils; thank you for my dress and for my hat. Thank you for making us this home." She nestled deep into him.

Peter finally stood up and asked what we were supposed to do. Nils whispered, "Well, there are two beds up there, one for each of you. Go pick one out and you boys can go get some sleep." We didn't need to be told twice. We each had our own bed!

Peter and I raced up the stairs and into the smaller of the two rooms. Peter took the bed by the window, and I gladly took the one near the door. Mine would be warmer. I sat on my own bed, gingerly at first, testing it a bit and, then, allowing myself to become heavier and heavier.

Peter propped himself up on his elbow. "Can you believe it? I never thought we would have our own house! I think Mama was so excited and happy, she just got tired."

I wasn't sure why Mama was so tired. I nodded, though. I never dreamed we would have our own house with my own bed. I climbed under the blanket and as I fell asleep, I thought how life was full of surprises. Just that morning, Peter and I had gone off to school not knowing we would move. Now, here we were, sleeping in our own beds. Nils was with our Mama, and she didn't have to work for Mr. Joclav anymore. The biggest surprise was how quiet our home was.

There was no trolley clanging past. Our rooms weren't filled with people yelling and laughing and cursing. There was just the four of us, all quiet in our neat little square.

First Love

Nils changed our lives more than we ever imagined possible. His hard work with Burlington Railroad paid off. He provided the four of us with a good life. We weren't wealthy, but it felt as if we were. After all, only a year prior we had one room for three.

Nils was completely taken with Mama. She was beautiful. As I grew, I noticed how many people took extra notice of her as she walked down the street. She was tall and slender and kept her hair in thick braids encircling her head. She had a graceful face. It was nearly perfectly symmetrical had the end of her nose not been slightly off to the right. Her wide, blue eyes sparkled with intellect and happiness. She was confident and assured of her importance in the world. Hard life hadn't broken her as it often does to many. Instead, it strengthened her and it showed in every aspect of her. Her wide mouth stretched into smiles effortlessly. Her teeth were stained, but her lips were so rosy red I don't think anyone noticed her teeth. Nils certainly didn't.

He worked hard to make her happy. When he got home, he raced to her. He picked her up hugging her to him and kissed her face and neck. He touched her hair and held her hand when they walked places. He showed her off proudly, always introducing her as "the most wonderful woman I ever met, my wife, Kat." Mama liked the extra attention, I could tell. Her cheeks were rosy and her eyes brighter than I had seen in a long time.

She loved the little home Nils bought for us and she always worked to keep it clean and beautiful. It was a typical home for the day. It wasn't stuffed with treasures. A few precious items adorned a set of shelves in the living room and our best vase sat in the middle of our table. It was a happy place, filled with love and growing us boys into fit young men.

Mama took great pride in the whole place and especially loved the garden. Nils dug a large part of the yard into fine straight rows. We all helped Mama plant cabbages, beans, squash, onions, and carrots each spring. I loved the magic of the growing plants. I eagerly watched for seedlings to break through the earth. After no time at all, they stretched into flower bearing plants. Mama loved the harvest. She always told us it would feed us all winter and then ensured it would. She canned everything. Her sauerkraut and pickles were my favorite. After the jars were all sealed, she lined them neatly on narrow shelves in our pantry. She loved feeding us and called us her "uprawy chłopców."

When Mama and Nils celebrated their two-year wedding anniversary, I noticed just how much Peter and I had grown. Peter was now taller than Mama. As usual, I was close behind and by the end of the year, I had grown taller than not only Mama, but Nils and Peter as well. Mama told me it was all in my legs.

That fall, I entered into high school, nothing more than a gangly wayward youth, clumsily tripping through life and happiest when I was fishing and trapping. The country was gripped with depression and even though Nils had a good job, our family struggled alongside everyone else. Mama was still grateful for the extra food Peter and I brought home each day.

It was a turning point for the entire world. The path before us was strewn with idealization. People idealized the perfect life, the perfect family and only two short decades later, the fifties realized this idealization. Behind us, revered traditions idealized proper manners, hard work, and religious belief. We were caught in a turbulent turning tide that produced the greatest generation. I didn't take too much notice; all I was learning was hard work was needed to survive life.

Peter and I trapped every day and, through the years, had built ourselves a respectable practice. We had several customers who relied on us. Mama relied on us to bring food to the table each day. Most days we caught enough fish to feed the four of us, and other days, Mama served up the rabbits caught in our traps. Nils told us every day how he was proud of us, and Peter and I didn't worry too much about school.

We couldn't skip out on high school as we had in our grammar school days with Miss Fink. High school classes were serious and Mama was adamant we would graduate. Peter struggled, just like before, and even though school wasn't my favorite place to be, I found I enjoyed it. Beside a fine academic education, there were girls.

Girls were mysterious for Peter and I. Mama never had another child after Rosie, so it was just us two boys. Most of our friends had sisters, but I never knew them. When we were younger, they were bossy, telling us to wash up and to be careful as if they were our mothers. They didn't like war games. I steered clear of most girls until that summer.

Peter still nursed a soft spot for Victoria and it turned out that she had a younger sister, Clara. She was younger, prettier, and smarter than Victoria, and I was smitten from the moment I first saw her.

Clara was unlike any other girl I had ever known. She was short with golden hair that looked soft. She had wide brown eyes, and her cheeks were slightly full. For whatever reason, she decided to be my friend, and we talked every day when Peter and I stopped at Smith's.

By that fall, I found myself thinking of Clara most of the day every day. She was curious about me and listened when I said anything. I knew she was smart, smarter than me; she could add in her head and she read any book she saw. She never acted like she was smarter than me or anyone else, though. She asked to follow us on our trapping line and was unappalled when she found the traps full. Instead, she asked what the next step was and then the next. She was learning to trap and genuinely wanted to do it well. She was the same with fishing. She wasn't very good at either sport, but I liked having her around, and when she wasn't, my day was just a little sad.

I wanted to do something nice for her but I really didn't know what I could do. Peter was no help—he talked to a lot of girls but never seemed to be serious about any of them. He talked to them, and I knew he kissed several, but after that, he moved on. Plus, he never made any progress with Victoria. She looked at him as if he were a child or worse, a younger brother.

It was different with Clara and me. She was happy to see me and never laughed at how short my pants were. I looked forward to just hearing her soft voice. I wanted to show her how much I thought of her but, for a few weeks, I had no idea what to do or even how to plan something nice. The only person I ever gave a present to was Mama. I finally decided to ask Miss Kate.

It had been awhile since I had seen her. After we moved out of that building, it was like our lives were just different and we hardly saw most people who had once been part of our daily routines. Peter and I stopped by a few times throughout the year to say our hellos and check in on her and Miss Vicki. Our chats were always short but became more sporadic as the years went by.

It had been a full year since I last visited our first home in Sheridan. I was myself excited to talk with Miss Kate. She was the first pretty girl I knew and liked and she was always nice to me. I think she figured out my crush on her but she didn't seem to mind. She still talked about moving to San Francisco and she still had her eastern accent. Going into that rear kitchen door felt like going home. It creaked familiarly and the smell of food engulfed me as I went through.

It didn't take long to find Miss Kate. She was doing dishes in the large sink and threw her arms around me when she saw me, dripping water all over my shirt.

"You're so tall, Jurak! How did this happen? You got all handsome on me and all grown up! Here, sit, sit down over there, I'll bring some tea." She pointed me to the nook I once took every meal of my day in, but someone had added a small table with two chairs filling the small space, making it more comfortable. I was too tall to put my legs beneath that table, so I sat sideways waiting for her and feeling awkward.

She came bustling back, and I admired how pretty she still was. Her hair was still short and shining ebony. Her face was slightly lined. Her eyes wrinkled at the edges even when she wasn't smiling now, but they still sparkled. I noticed how fine her legs were and how short her dress was. I tried not to stare as she sat opposite me.

"So, what brings ya here, hun?"

I couldn't remember. I picked up my cup of tea and desperately tried to recall what had prompted me to visit. I was keenly aware of how close she sat and how good she smelled. I drank my tea and watched her over the rim of my cup.

"It's all same old, same old 'round here. We had a big fight the other night, and Mr. Joclav kicked out several of our girls. I dunno where they went." She talked, in her normal way, too much about everything going on in the building until a crash from around the corner interrupted us. She peeked around the corner. When she turned around, her face was white.

"Hun, you go on upstairs, I'll be there in a minute." She handed me a key to a room.

I don't know what frightened her and I didn't ask, I just followed her directions and left the kitchen in the opposite direction of the noise. I ran up the stairs and down the same hall we had lived in, stopping in front of a door that was supposed to be marked 24 but no numbers hung there any longer.

Stepping inside, I realized I was in Miss Kate's room. It was small, furnished with a bed, dresser, and radiator. It was cluttered, she obviously had done her wash the night prior, and the fresh smell of the powder lingered in the air. Her bed was untidy, the quilt hastily pulled into place, and the pillows carelessly tossed on top. A cord, strung diagonally across the room held her sensitive clothing. I tried not to look at those items while I waited. On top of the dresser, she had a small stack of books. I looked through those, curious what Miss Kate would read about. They all seemed to take place next to the ocean in San Francisco.

The doorknob turned, and I quickly dropped the books back where I found them. Miss Kate hurried in and locked the door behind her. "He's getting meaner, I swear. He forgets things and hits more than he used to. He was always a bad man, but I swear I can hardly be around anymore! His business is failing, and I dunno what we are all going to do if he goes under. I'm gunna have to talk with Pearl; you know her? Up the street? Everyone likes her, and I think her beds are nicer and rooms bigger than here anyways," Miss Kate talked the whole time she crossed the small room to her bed and sat on it. She patted the space next to her. "Sit here, hun, and tell me why you're here."

Now, I had never been alone in any room with any woman before this. I followed her direction, though, and tried to act natural as I sat far away from her on that old bed. It sank under my weight causing her to lean towards me. I put my hands in my lap and looked to the floor. Miss Kate seemed to change tune, just then and she moved closer to me, rubbing my arm with both her hands.

"Why did you come, Jurak? Ya miss me? I always knew you liked me more than you said." Her voice was soft and flirty, and I couldn't answer. I reached out to one of those pretty legs and rubbed as high as I dared, just above her knee. She tilted her face up to mine, looked in my eyes, and kissed my mouth; we never broke eye contact, and I was breathing hard.

I put my arms around her small shoulders and pulled myself close into her. She wrapped her legs around my waist and let me lean over her on that bed.

It didn't last long, but I was in heaven and completely spent after. She lay there holding my hand. "See? I knew you liked me."

It was then, laying there on her bed, her head resting on my shoulder, I remembered why I had come here that day. "I do like you, Miss Kate. I always did." I wasn't shy anymore. "I know you can help me too. There's a girl, Clara. I really like her and I want to do something nice for her."

Miss Kate laughed quietly. "I'm guessin' she's not ready for what we just did, is she?"

I thought about what she said, "I don't think we are ready for that, no."

She laughed at my earnestness, "You remember your teeth? When you lost 'em and were so upset, you thought you were a man? Well, you're a man now, but I can't expect you to know how to treat a girl proper just yet. Tell me about this girl, and I can tell you what to do."

So, I told her all about Clara, how short she was and how beautiful she was, how she was smart and seemed to like the outdoors as much as I did. I told her she worked at Smith's and that she got good grades. Miss Kate never interrupted and just listened until I finished.

She sighed after, the saddest sigh I think I had ever heard. "She sounds real nice, Jurak, real nice. If I had a nice young man, someone as nice as you, I'd want to know. Have ya told her yet?" I shook my head even though I knew Miss Kate couldn't see me, but she felt it. "That's what I thought. Ya need to tell her, Jurak. What good is love if you don't share it? You get her some flowers from your mama's garden and take her for a walk. Take her somewhere pretty, the prettiest spot you know. Then, just tell her what ya told me. I think you'll do just fine."

It was a simple plan, and I liked it. Miss Kate had been the right one to talk to. "Ya gotta go? Anything you want before ya leave?" Her voice was soft and in my ear. The second time was better.

Afterwards, I left walking down the hallway a bit taller. I was glad I had gone to see Miss Kate.

The simple plan she devised turned out to be difficult. It took me a whole week and three bunches of flowers, before I could meet up with Clara. Something held me back and I visited Miss Kate one more time before I felt brave enough to approach Clara.

She was just finishing up work when I walked in with the flowers. She seemed surprised to see me but pleased as well and she gladly took the flowers.

"Did you get these from your mama's garden, Jurak? They're beautiful." She held them close to her nose taking in their sweet fragrance.

"I was just going for a walk, will you come with me?" I asked hopefully through a tight throat. She looked up into my eyes and smiled, walking to my right as we ambled down the road.

We were quiet for a time—the flowers made us both shy. One of the best things about Clara was the fact she didn't have to talk all the time; she was content to just take in the world around her and quietly contemplate life. We walked out of town, towards the creek, the prettiest spot I knew.

We sat side by side on the bank and watched day turn to dusk. "Clara, you're the nicest girl I know. You're smart, you're funny, and I think you are the prettiest person I ever saw." It wasn't eloquent and it all came out in a rush, but I was sincere, and she knew it.

She grinned. "Jurak, are you telling me you like me?" I nodded. She took my hand then and we watched the sun sink lower into the sky. She kept smiling and I knew I was too. I led her back to town and there, in front of Smith's, I leaned down and kissed her on her cheek. She gasped and looked around.

"Careful, someone might see us!" I could tell she liked it, though, and I wasn't too worried about who might see us.

She kissed me back, quickly. "See you tomorrow, Jurak," she said and walked away, holding the flowers close to her chest.

I was walking on clouds that night and even stopped by our garden to pick a flower for our own dinner table. Mama took one look at me and knew something was up. "Something is up, Jurak, tell me what it is. All week you have been a little different."

Peter looked closely at me and grinned. I had told him all about Miss Kate the day it happened. Mama wasn't talking about that, though. She was talking about today and the change she saw in me now. I wasn't ready to tell her about Clara just yet, though.

I gave her the flower I picked, and she thanked me by reminding me to wash up for dinner. Nils came in and we washed next to each other. Mama put dinner on the table and we all sat down. I looked around our family and felt life would never be better.

A few days went by, and I didn't see Clara at all. I got busy and she was busy; it was bound to happen but it still saddened me. After school, I let Peter run ahead to our trapping line and I stopped by Smith's. Victoria was there, but I couldn't see Clara. Victoria came out the door.

"She's sick, real sick, Jurak." Her voice was pinched, afraid and I felt that pinching feeling deep in my stomach that I had almost forgotten. She didn't wait for me to answer, just went back into the shop, leaving me wondering what was making Clara so sick.

I went out to our trapping line but my heart wasn't in it, and Peter just sent me to the creek telling me I was better at fishing anyways. It was true, I was good at fishing. Even when I was sad, I was good at fishing and it was no different today. By the time Peter caught up to me, I had caught enough for our dinner and enough for Aunt Anya's family too.

Peter asked me about Clara on our walk back to town but there wasn't too much to tell. I didn't know why she was sick. Peter tried cheering me up all the way back reminding me of Miss Kate, but I felt far away and didn't pay too much attention to my brother. We dropped Aunt Anya's share of fish off with their family and headed home.

Mama was happy to have the fish, as usual and while she finished dinner, I told her all about Clara. Mama never interrupted but her eyes grew serious when I mentioned she was sick. Mama took sicknesses very seriously, and I could tell she was as worried as I.

A few days went by and I didn't see Victoria or Clara when I walked by Smith's. I had no idea what happened to them and the one time I asked the guy behind the counter, he just shrugged. A whole week went by before we heard about the sisters.

Clara's father had caught the flu a few weeks before, and of course, everyone in their family had fallen ill because of the illness. Victoria was the last to get it, right after I had seen her. Both girls ran high fevers and instead of recovering after a few days as their father had, they grew worse.

Both girls died the same afternoon a week after Clara had fallen ill. By the time I heard the news, Clara was already buried.

Peter and I walked home, heads down, in complete silence. There was nothing to say.

Graduation

When I learned about Clara, life stopped for a little while, as with any loss it does. At first, each day knowing she was gone was empty but the days kept coming and eventually filled up. I kept learning and fishing, but a part of my life stopped. I didn't seek out any other girl; I didn't visit Miss Kate anymore. Peter was the opposite.

Peter and I had always been different as most brothers are. I was tall, he was short. He was incredibly good at school and learning. It took me a while to catch on. My hair was like Mama's, dark and curly. Peter's was lighter. Peter was fun, I was more serious. We approached the loss of our girls in very different manners.

Unlike me, life didn't stop for Peter. Instead of shying away from girls, he warmed up to them more than ever and he acquired quite the reputation. Mama admonished him, Nils tried to guide him, but Peter never did listen. Every Saturday, Peter was out late and one weekend, a month or so after Clara, he invited me.

I spent most days with my brother trapping and fishing, but I had never spent a Saturday night with him.

Though Peter and I shared many friends, I didn't know most of his weekend crowd well. They were rougher than my friends, always wanting to have a good time and most of them didn't have jobs.

There were around fifteen boys and girls that met, unofficially, outside a saloon at the edge of town. That saloon was known for questionable activity. All were welcome, no matter the class, no matter the color, no matter the language they spoke, all were welcome. Unless they were Indian. No Native Americans were allowed inside, but the entrance was always crowded with Indians hoping for a drink. Peter led us inside and we sat at a couple of tables and someone brought out some cards.

I was excited to try my hand at what I was sure to be a winning night. The night did not start out well. I was a novice to drinking having only had a couple of drinks here and there, but Peter was an expert. Before we even began the game, he threw back two shots and laughed loudly, winking at a girl who I think they called Bella.

Bella was not known as a nice girl, though everyone in her group liked her. She was the only daughter of one of the black workers from downtown. She was brown, curvy, and strong. I believed her when she told me she would move to New York City. No matter what that girl did, she was good at it, and I was sure singing in New York City would be no different. That night, I learned she was good at singing, drinking, and winning any card game. After only thirty minutes, my pockets were empty, and I had nothing to show for my Saturday night. I was so broke, I couldn't even buy my own drink. I was left waiting for my brother the rest of the night. We didn't get home until nearly 3 a.m.

Mama didn't believe in letting us sleep in— Sundays were for church, no matter and most probably in spite of, coming in so late. Peter followed us all the way to the church, eyes down, shoulders slumped. He stopped twice, heaving last night's fun into various gardens. Mama kept her shoulders squared and eyes forward, firmly ignoring his state.

Bella and Peter enjoyed each other last night, that much I knew. After she took my money at cards, she took my brother out to the back. I truly didn't mind. After all, fun was fun, but Peter was acting strange this morning. Something other than a bad hangover was bothering him.

His gait was awkward and when we sat at our usual seat, he couldn't keep still. I noticed Nils paid special attention to him. Finally, and thankfully, without a word, Nils got up and led him away. Mama's mouth thinned but she never spoke a word. We walked home, and she made us lunch.

"What did you boys get up to last night? Drinking? Girls?"

"Yes," I answered honestly, not sure how to talk to my mother about last night. Peter always went out Saturday nights, so I wasn't sure what Mama knew or guessed about his activities.

She just shook her head and talked about her garden. I helped clear the table and brought her a cup of tea. It made her happy, I could tell. She patted my cheek and thanked me.

Peter and Nils came home soon after, Mama told Peter dinner was over, but she made Nils a plate. Peter and I went outside and walked down to the creek. He grinned, chagrined.

"What happened to you?" Witnessing his discomfort during service had piqued my curiosity. I knew something was wrong but had no idea what plagued my brother.

"Well, Nils took me to see Doc Brown. Thank God for Nils, Jurak. He knew what was wrong. I never had to ask for help, but it was the worst itching I ever had. He knew what to do and you know Nils, he didn't ask too many questions." I didn't ask any more questions either. Peter never got with Bella again.

I went out with Peter every Saturday after that. Even though I was the younger brother, I watched over and helped him home each night. Each Sunday morning, I got him up and dressed. Peter just liked having a good time, and I wasn't too shabby at it either. The rest of the school year passed, and Peter graduated from high school despite all our fun, the trapping line, and all our fishing.

It was strange after that. Peter worked a few jobs around town. Nils had a couple of friends who farmed, and Peter helped hay all that fall. He kept up our trapping line, and I found myself on my own more than ever before.

It was around June we began really hearing about Europe. Mama was especially interested in that news as she still had family in Austria and Poland who had already suffered through the First World War. After she worried about her family so far away, she turned her attentions to us, her sons. She repeatedly told Nils she hadn't raised us to die. Nils listened, patient as always, but the world was what it was—he couldn't stop her from worrying. Nils couldn't prevent war.

Just like the rest of the country, Sheridan wasn't for the war. Most people were just trying to survive from meager paycheck to meager paycheck, keeping their large families fed. War in Europe was far away and not as threatening as starving. No one wanted war.

We got through fall, and 1941 dawned. I was up for graduation, ready to leave school behind. I had no idea what I was going to do but I knew I was done with that classroom setting. I was a young man, raring to make my life, my fortune, and 1941 was the year to do it.

Graduation was a simple affair, but Mama made a fuss. She made a little cake to celebrate and Aunt Anya's family came by. Uncle Antonin offered me a job. He said the coalmine was always looking for strong young men to clear away rubble. I wasn't too sure about mining deep in the earth but clearing away rubble sounded safe. I thanked him, and the small party broke up soon after.

Peter and I walked down to the creek, poles in hands, hoping for a good catch. Looking out over the water I felt that pinching feeling once more, deep inside my stomach. One chapter of my life was done; there was no going back, and I felt a tremendous sense of loss. I knew it would pass with time and my new life would make sense soon enough. I had no idea where I was headed or where life would lead me, but I felt ready.

Training

That summer was the best. Peter got me work right alongside him. Half the summer we worked cattle and the other we worked horses. The horses belonged to a Scotch family who bred world-renowned polo and military horses. I enjoyed working the horses best of the two jobs. I found the cattle work mundane. Cows were slow, stupid, and big, but the work paid well and gave me a place to live the whole summer.

We still fished and ran our trapping line. We were too busy to go everyday but every weekend we were, went back to our favorite haunts, back to what we did best. We stayed at home Friday night through Sunday and ate Mama's good food. We followed her to church and helped Nils around the house. Mama's flowerbeds yielded the best flowers in town. She was generous with her colorful crop and every neighbor had cuttings growing in their own yards that started from her humble beginnings.

The summer went too fast and as fall approached, the world waited to see how the United States would respond to the war in Europe. Hitler was taking over Europe and, in our house, this was discussed nearly every day, even without new news.

Mama discussed the events, daily, in a frantic mix of language with Aunt Anya. They wondered how their siblings, cousins, and parents were holding up under Nazi rule. Mama prayed as she went about her daily tasks non-stop. Her brother had been killed during the first year of the Great War, and she despaired over the idea her family would face more war desperation.

I felt closer, somehow, to her homeland, than ever before. She raised Peter and me with her traditions and language. We knew all her childhood stories by heart. I could picture her homeland more clearly than ever before.

The village was old, with cobbled streets I could almost feel under my feet as she spoke. I could see the neat town square and small, beloved homes lining the streets. It scared me how close something so far away was becoming in my mind.

As summer turned to fall, the European situation worsened. It was 1941, and Europe raged with war that no one except Germany had desired. Hitler invaded Poland and Czechoslovakia with no apparent resistance. His attempts to conquer France were one step too far, though, and the crisis of war had rapidly unfolded, quickly escalating to a point of no return. The United States resisted strong European urges to aid or join in the fight.

I was swept up in the emotion of watching it all unfold. I knew my place in the world and strongly desired Hitler would be stopped, however, I did not desire to fight. I knew how my uncle had died. Mama's brother had inhaled a poisonous, noxious gas that truly frightened me. When Peter and I were small, Mama expressed gratitude for our humble situation because we, at the very least, we were not surviving ramifications of a war that had taken her brother and nearly starved her cousins. War frightened me. Especially the talk of such widespread death. I could only too clearly see all those people lying in their cold holes in the ground, left lonely in lonely places.

I didn't want to leave my home. I loved the mountains I lived in and only felt truly alive when I was in them. I appreciated every tree, rock, and gulley as I walked and fished my way. I had no desire to leave them behind, even if for a short time. I was like any other young man who craved adventure and recognition, but deep down, my soul was content.

December 7, 1941 hit fast and hard, bringing that pinching feeling of reality back to my gut. The United States no longer had a choice to stay apart from world affairs as the Japs dragged us into it. Mama was terrified as Peter and I filled out draft cards, praying and crying the entire time.

Peter kissed her forehead, "Don't worry so much, Mama. When the U.S. joins, the war will be over before you know it." Watching my mother dry her eyes, I couldn't help but hope he was right.

We submitted our cards early in the New Year. The United States responded to the attacks on Pearl Harbor by sending troops to both Europe and Asia. I was anxious to go as young men from our hometown waited orders. I felt this was my duty, like it or not. I never mentioned my fears to anyone else, pushing them deep down past the pinching feeling in my gut. Peter talked big, especially to young women, calling on their sympathies for a young man facing the tragedies of war.

Soon enough, we were both called up. Peter left first. He was ordered to basic training and follow on orders to a new division in the Colorado Rockies. He would receive specifics later.

I was ordered to Fort Benning, a base located in Georgia. I had no idea what to expect but as time drew nearer, I began hearing how tough basic training really was. I wasn't too worried—I was in great shape and was even used to early mornings, both thanks to the hard ranch work I performed since high school graduation.

The day I boarded that bus taking me so far from the only life I knew and understood, I fought hard to keep back my tears. Mama held me too tight and covered my face in tears and kisses. Aunt Anya came to say her goodbyes. Loud as ever, she cried as she told me goodbye, cried as I walked away, and cried to my mother that we just grew too quickly. Mama was quiet, her shoulders shaking and hands clutching for Nils and Anya. As I waved from my seat, I realized how small Mama was. Nils held her up, and Anya waved to me. All of Mama's children were now gone. I wished, once more, Rosie had survived. Blinking back my own tears and fears, I waved again and then focused my attentions to my journey ahead of me.

I had been excited to board that bus, to see another part of the country but soon realized how long and terribly boring riding a bus across the United States was. Mostly, I slept. I talked with my neighbors, and when we stopped, I gratefully stretched, but most of the ride was uneventful. It took four days and three drivers to get across the country.

The first time I stepped onto Georgia soil, I was overwhelmed by the humidity. It was June and already, the heat was intense. Instantly, I felt a trickle of sweat making its way down my back. My lungs balked at the heavy air, and I found it difficult to breath. It was so humid, I could see the haze of water hanging in the air before me—I could taste it. I did not like it.

Then I was introduced to my drill sergeant, Sergeant Rust. He was fit, only a few years older than me and though was shorter, he was so intense he invoked fear and respect from his new recruits. He called us to order, and we obeyed. He was not a man to disobey.

"Welcome to Jump School. My name is Sergeant Rust. I am sure we will get to know each other well over the next few weeks. I doubt most of you will make it— none of you looks smart enough, and I bet most of you are wishing you were already home with your mama's."

As he spoke, he wandered through our group, leaning in too close, glaring deep into our eyes. His voice was low but carried a threat he was yet to utter. I kept my eyes forward as anxiety filled my body and soul.

Sergeant Rust wore the army fatigues, stretched over his fit frame, showing off muscles I wasn't sure I had, no matter how many hours I'd spent working at the ranch.

"It is my job to provide the army with the best soldiers trained in the art of war, ready to fight the Krauts. I can see I have been given the impossible task. None of you will make it; this training is only for the elite, and I can't think why I see so many young men in front of me with zero ability to complete this training." With each word, his voice grew harsher and louder. "You can leave. In fact, leave now. There is no shame in leaving now." He stood in front of me now. "Leave. I know men and I know you are not strong enough or smart enough for jump school. You will never wear the wings." He was practically shouting at my face, every word articulated ensuring I understood his warning and threat. I didn't want to wash out my first day. He stood in front me, glaring into my eyes, daring me to back down. I stared straight ahead, more afraid than I ever felt before, but I kept my place in the line.

After that, we counted off by two's and organized ourselves into messy lines, marching off to retrieve our uniforms, get our haircuts, and stop for lunch. We were ordered not to talk and a grim determination settled over us as we did as we were ordered. Lines, I realized, were an important part of the military lifestyle. Hurry up and wait. Hurry up and wait. I followed as best as I could. I took my uniform, sat through my haircut, and hurried through the chow line, all without talking once. I listened as Sergeant Rust ordered us, berated us, and promised us Hell. It was a terribly long day, and by dinnertime, the moral in our group was low.

I missed home. That clean, clear air, crispy and abundant in my lungs was the first thing I thought of when I finally lay down on a top bunk. The night air was as hot as the day and soon, my clothes and bedclothes were wet from my sweat and the air. I missed my freedoms and my mama. I missed Peter. Somehow, I held it together that night, but I could hear the strange gulping sounds penetrate the night as others succumbed to our fate. Morning dawned too early. We ran to breakfast. Then, we ran to calisthenics and to judo training. After that, we ran to the field for shooting. I ran everywhere, every day. It was exhausting and nearly unbearable that first week. All the while, we remained silent, only speaking when spoken to and listening to Sergeant Rust critique our every move.

He promised us more Hell as we progressed and a few washed out. He made good on every single promise and by week four, I was so busy, I nearly forgot life before training.

I missed home, but I was so busy I couldn't stop to think about that. I missed eating meals at the normal leisurely pace meant, but I was too hungry to take the time to care. Everyday went by in a blur of anxiety and hard work.

I learned to obey without argument or thought to argue. My body hardened with muscle. By the time we began jumping, I believed I was ready for anything.

Our first jump was from a two-hundred-fifty-foot tower. I was given a parachute. I climbed the tower and hooked up. Then, I looked down. It was so high, the ground seemed unreal. My fear dissolved, and I jumped. Every single one of us made our jump. Our next jump was more difficult and more than a few hardened men washed out.

Sergeant Rust didn't give us any direction or idea of what to expect. We did our morning run and headed out to the field. We ran right past the two-hundred-fifty-foot tower towards the back of the field. There, in front of us, was a short tower with a wooden box at the top.

The box looked like part of an airplane with a narrow entryway. I estimated the whole tower to stand about thirty feet high. I joined the line in front of my newest obstacle. I was wondering how the Hell a chute could operate on such short notice. It seemed impossible.

Sergeant Rust informed us there was no chute. Instead, we would jump from the tower towards the ground, connected to a cable that would save us just before we hit. After his abrupt explanation, it looked even more impossible. We hooked up and began our climb. By the time we reached the top I was sure the cable would never hold.

I stepped into that makeshift plane and was hit with air so musty and so full of the smell of dirty men, I gagged. I heard people coughing and gasping as they encountered this challenge we hadn't anticipated. The world closed in around me, and I desperately wanted out. I made my way to the door, questioning my own logic and especially the army's.

"Whose idea was this? They want to kill us all before the war? Fuck." Apparently, I wasn't the only one worried about the potential outcome.

The line moved slowly forward. Then, a guy pushed by me, choosing to climb down rather than face the jump. Another guy pushed by me, followed by another, then another. I could logically conclude some had completed their jump but the windows were angled wrong, making it impossible to see anyone walking away. There was no way to know if or how many were injured during this jump. Somehow, I kept walking towards that door. I checked my cable, the guy behind me checked it again, and out I went.

It happened faster than I could even think. I felt a terrible jerk in my groin area that I was sure would bruise and hit the ground, hard, nearly simultaneously. My breath was knocked out of me but I had done it. I graduated from jump school soon after.

Everyone earned a weekend pass the week after graduation. I was a different man. Even my appearance had changed—I stood straighter and my body was void of any fat. I was excited to finally experience Georgia. I looked forward to Southern girls. So far, I hated Georgia and had only seen the base.

My hometown, Sheridan, was actually diverse and accepting, thanks to the mining camps and people's desire to grow a better life. Luckily, I had grown up with colored kids, Chinese kids, and all the rest, never questioning their worth. There were no segregation laws and men took their hats off to all women, black or white. Georgia was completely segregated.

Not long after I left the base, I realized black folks refused to look me in the eye. As we passed each other on the street, they looked down and stepped out of my way. I had never had a lady or old men move out of my way. I felt myself staring, but I couldn't help it.

I followed my friend, Taylor, up the road to a bar. On the door was a small sign that clearly stated 'NO BLACKS.' I couldn't believe it. Here we were, fighting a white devil while denying good people a Goddamned drink. I left town, making my way back to the base. I was disappointed in Georgia.

I wanted to leave and got my wish. A few days after my weekend pass, I found myself on my way towards North Carolina. It was further north, but it felt the same. It was still oppressively hot and humid. It was severely segregated. I added Glider Pilot School to my resume, and then received my orders overseas.

My unit was ordered to French Morocco, Africa. I was surprised, and most of us couldn't understand how we were going to Africa when the real fight was in Europe. During our entire jump school, we were cut off from most news from the rest of the world. No war updates penetrated to distract us from our training. At night, we talked and theorized but no one had any real answers. Morocco was an excellent staging area. It was only ninety miles from the shores of Italy, making it the best waiting zone, protected, far away from danger, but Europe was near enough. Never in my wildest imaginings had I ever thought I would find myself in Africa. Never.

Unfeeling to my consternation, the Army Air Corps ordered us to prepare. After just a few days, I joined a line to board the ship that would take me across the Atlantic. More than a few of us worried aloud about German U-boats. I worried as much as anyone but I had never seen an ocean before. For a while, all I could do was wonder at the vast amount of water that surrounded me. I wanted to fish, to catch the big one from deep below us but, of course, I had no tackle.

I spent as much time as I could on deck, no matter the weather. I had no desire to be caught below in case of attack and I enjoyed the ocean air on my face. While on the ship, we stuck to our severe training schedule and silence. I was extremely relieved when we made it to French Morocco.

Landing there, I was strongly reminded of the American south. It was hot and humid. I could stand the humidity after my months of training but I missed the crisp mountain air. We set up living quarters best as we could and immediately began speculating how long we would be there. No one was eager to sit around or continue training. We admired ourselves, the brave soldiers we had become. There was no doubt it would be us that would stop Hitler.

We acted as if we were already in theatre. We ate from our own mess kits, washing them best as we could when we finished. Our beds were little more than cots and even the latrines were made to move. Everything, our entire world, felt ready and poised for the action we had so ardently trained for.

Most of us took time to write letters home— who knew how long we would have the time for letter writing. I told Mama and Nils all about training and segregation. I told them all about the ocean, even though both them had crossed the same one. I told Mama I missed her and her cooking and I meant it. I wrote Peter and poked slight fun at him for still training while I was headed out. And too soon, the call for action found us.

That last night in Morocco, Taylor and I found a way to town and drank to life. Girls surrounded us American GI's and were only too giving for American money. No one said too much to any of us—we were headed to war.

Sicily

Jumping was terrifying. I never found it thrilling. I hated it but I did my duty, feeling a desire deep in my soul to succeed that I could never fully understand. All through training, I was inspired to do better, especially when I saw good men wash out. There was nothing so difficult jumping into the dark abyss of the night sky, trusting only in my chute. Every jump I made, I did it without thinking. Sicily was no different; I simply fell into the open sky, mind as blank as possible. I readied my body for the jerk of my chute. Out of nowhere, I felt something was off. I crashed into the earth and my gut instinct guided me to take cover.

There was chaos and plenty of firing, but that didn't make sense. The Sicilian shores were almost void of any Nazis, thanks to Operation Mincemeat. The operation, which had worked more than ever hoped, was devised by the Brits. During the months leading up to our invasion, a plan was thought up and carried out. It began in Wales and ended in Spain.

They needed a body. A male in his late thirties was preferred. They needed someone no one would miss. A man, with no family and no ties to his home was sought. After a few failed attempts, they finally found the perfect guy—Glyndwyr Michael.

They found him in an abandoned warehouse in Wales. He'd been dead a few days from ingesting rat poison. He was unemployed and on his own. No one knew if he ate the poison on purpose or out of hunger. They removed the body and shipped him out for the next phase of the plan.

They dressed him as Royal Marine in, possibly, the nicest suit poor Glyndwyr ever wore. His pockets were stuffed with personal identification naming him Captain William Martin. As a finishing touch, they handcuffed a briefcase to his hand that was full of fake documents. Those detailed a planned invasion, naming Greece and Sardinia as starting points and Sicily as a feint. Next, the poor bastard was dropped into the sea off the coast of Spain with high hopes the German navy would find him. The plan worked better than clockwork.

The guy was found and the documents read. Both the body and documents were reported right up the chain, all the way to Hitler. Hitler was never convinced the plan was nothing more than a ruse and ordered all his troops to Sardinia and Greece. The Nazis even buried Captain William Martin beneath a plaque in Spain. It was the perfect plan, with the perfect outcome, except...

The United States Navy had never fully been notified of the 82nd Airborne parachute drop. Friendly fire took out over three hundred 504's before we were even out of the sky. We knew war was Hell but we had never trained to expect such animosity from our own. Someone, somewhere stopped the Navy, but there was blood and bodies everywhere. Guys hopelessly tangled up in their chutes with limbs and heads bent at every unimaginable, terrible angle, their eyes stuck open.

I met the ground with every muscle in my body taut, ready for action. Every sense I had improved as I listened for any new noises. I looked for signs of danger. I was now a soldier. Later, I acknowledged there'd been the briefest moment of change during that fall to earth. Before the drop I was just a kid from Wyoming, ready for action. After that drop, I was a soldier.

I rallied around and somehow found my friend, Taylor. We walked, together to the pre-set meeting point. We saw a few Germans running northeast, but they were too far away. The chaos of friendly fire finally ceased, and the night filled with sounds of the ocean, distant yells, and just a few rounds of fire here and there.

When we finally reached the rallying point, we saw cleanup of the beach already taking place. Those poor guys who hadn't made it through the jump, were being pulled from the water and untangled from their chutes. Their lives wasted, without even witnessing battle.

Taylor whispered, "There's going to be Hell to pay for this," I could only nod.

The first days in Sicily were wonderful. We knew the fight was close, but all we experienced were grateful locals. We ate enough and the weather was perfect. All too soon, the peace ended.

We marched northwards, into Italy, in search of Nazis. I wondered if we would run into Peter.

He was part of the elite Mountain Division. They trained somewhere in the Rockies of Colorado, and, from his last letter, I gathered he was bored. The Mountain Division did some of the hardest training of the war. They learned ski and repel. There were no towns near them, and I wondered how in the Hell Peter survived without drink or women. I wrote him asking how he was and shared what I could, knowing the censors would black out anything that gave away our position or mission goals. In the end, I realized how much I couldn't tell him and ended up with only a few lines that felt empty for the relationship we once shared. I sent it off anyway and, for the first time since leaving the U.S., felt the enormity of the distance that separated myself from my family. I had no true idea where Peter was, just as he had no idea where I was.

Our battalion was given a rather vague objective of liberating Italy. The only option was victory. We were the heroes, the only ones left on God's green Earth, to end Hitler and his Nazi regime. I wondered if I would ever feel true freedom again.

It wasn't long before we found the fight. It turned out Nazis were fine fighters who also wanted to live. There were three young men before us and training took over before I realized what I was doing or what I was capable of when the first man went down. I had slit his throat. He knew it, he felt himself die. He reached for his throat, then out to me. I was already turning on the next. He looked me in the eye as I stabbed him with my bayonet. He hung there causing me to drop my rifle with his weight. A look of pain crossed over his face, a look like I had never seen. I felt his ribs crack. Years of trapping, freeing animals from pain caused an instinctive reaction from me. I shot, ending his pain. Taylor shot the third twice: Once in the chest and once in the head.

My bayonet was stuck in the young man. I hadn't expected that; it was hung up on his ribs, then muscle, and, as I pulled it free, strings of tissue came with the blade. It made me sick, and I threw up on the ground near him, splashing his tangled remains with my vomit. His left eye was closed but his right eye stayed open. I knew it wouldn't shut, so I put his arm over his face and turned away. Taylor was watching me.

I had no idea who the men were. They were German Nazis, that was all, I told myself but I knew better. They were sons, brothers, and schoolmates who would be forgotten. *At least it isn't cold*, I thought as we walked away.

Our push northward kept us so busy, we forgot to be tired. Locals moved out of our way, afraid we were the dangerous men. I couldn't see us that way. We were young men simply doing the job we had ardently trained for. As we cleared our way forward, we easily returned to being us; we were just young men, joking around, always ready for the next meal, and trying to find our way in a world gone mad.

Southern Italy turned difficult and as we moved north, closer to Europe, the fighting increased and grew tougher with each passing day. Our reputation preceded us, which was helpful. Once in a while, there were more surrendering than we killed.

Taylor told me the only good German was a dead one, and, at least during the war, it was true. The first group we let go, quickly returned to fight. There were four and we had nowhere to detain them. Two days later, we lived to regret that.

Taylor and I found ourselves alone one day. We were walking through a small field when we were ambushed. We never even heard them.

I noticed the similarities we shared. They were young, about our sizes and scarred shitless. They wanted to survive. We recognized each other from the day before, when we'd released them. I saw it in their eyes and though they spoke no English, I knew they understood when I shouted, "Hey!" They forced Taylor and I onto our knees, but when they went to take my weapon, my training kicked in.

I held onto my rifle and kicked out with my right leg, knocking one to the ground. Taylor hit another in the knees with his own weapon. Before the other two even registered that their buddies were on their backs, we had knocked them down, too. Taylor shot three of them, while I wrestled with the other and driving my hand into his throat, cutting off his air supply. I felt his throat in my hand a long time after the fight. Taylor and I never let anyone go again.

That same night, we got mail. I was tired. More tired than I had ever been. Training seemed a long time ago and even those hard days hadn't taken my energy like that day did. I found myself, laying on the ground as comfortably as if it was my own bed; I was that exhausted. My arm rested on my helmet and my other arm held onto my rifle. I let my eyes close but woke when I felt the pile of mail hit my midsection. There were three letters. I was too tired to even read them. I tucked them carefully into my shirt and went into a dreamless sleep.

We had a few hours respite the next morning. I took my much-needed shower and shaved. I ate breakfast as quickly as I'd been trained and read my letters. All of them were much longer than anything I'd sent out.

Peter was still in Colorado, ready to join the fight and bored even with all the repelling and climbing. I think he was stone sober and couldn't believe he liked that either.

Aunt Anya wrote a touching letter filled with summer news. She gardened with Mama and said she enjoyed it. She told me about a few changes throughout town. Miss Fink had finally married and would no longer be teaching. Juliet, Aunt Anya's youngest, was thinking of learning to teach and was a strong supporter of the war effort. She policed the family on rationing and blackouts, ever vigilant to do more than their part. Aunt Anya sounded proud of her. At the end, she instructed me to care for myself and watch out for the enemy. It made me smile—she was bossy as normal.

I saved Mama's letter for last. It even smelled like home. She always wrote a lot and today was no exception—there were three pages filled. She started by asking me how I was. I found the second page most interesting. She ran into Miss Kate who, as usual, told her all the gossip from our old home. Mr. Joclav was dead.

Miss Kate told Mama how it all happened. Apparently, he had been ill for quite a while with the most unsurprising diagnosis of syphilis. He nearly lost his business through his suffering and finally, Miss Vicki had taken over the running of everything. Miss Kate was proud to tell Mama how they all contributed to the war effort and helped "their boys." I could almost hear her New York accent.

She told Mama, Mr. Joclav had slipped into an unreal world of madness. He had spent his final years worsening, walking around the halls muttering to himself. For a while, he was more dangerous than ever, and Miss Kate stayed away from him as much as possible. His screams carried down the hallways late at night, and she told Mama how it unnerved her deep in her soul. She said it was strange to see such a man break.

Finally, one night, Miss Kate said it was a Thursday he ceased to exist. She heard him scream that night, more than ever before, and carried on for hours. She told Mama she knew it was bad that night and could feel death at her door. Mr. Joclav began running up and down the second-floor hall, right in front of our old door. It was the room with the radiator and he screamed Mama's name over and over again, mad with rage. He yelled about boys and cats and refused to calm. Then, he backed up against the far wall and ran, head down, straight into the door, breaking his own neck.

Mama never wrote if she was relieved or any other feelings about him. She and I never talked about him again. I knew we were all relieved though. The world was finally rid of a poison, and everyone knew Miss Vicki would do a better job of running that old building anyway.

I slept after I read my mother's words but, this time, I dreamt of trapped animals that evolved into Nazis. I woke, shaking, to see Taylor in front of me, telling me it was time to move out.

I didn't want to fight anymore. I had seen enough of war to last me a lifetime, and we had only been in theatre a few weeks. After my dream, though, I knew, without a doubt, we were fighting the good fight and could not lose. No Nazis would ever enter my hometown.

Anzio

Italy quickly turned into a terrible fight for survival each and every day. My training is all that saved me. I fought and even killed without second-guessing myself, without thinking what actions needed to come next. I quickly learned that fighting is just one horror of war. War is so much more than hunting and killing the enemy. I was shocked to learn that humans can live subjected to such horrible, demeaning circumstances.

Soldiers are displaced with no real place to rest. Each day, we faced the elements. We learned to ignore the heat, cold, rain, and snow. Continually being exposed to the elements made our skin calloused and red. Our hair grew longer than standard regulations, and we were generally grimy. Ironically, we tried to shave every day. Everyone battled bugs. They crawled through our clothes and hair. We changed and washed our clothes when we were able, but honestly, I always thought our numbers were doubled as our uniforms could have stood and fought on their own. We smelled so bad, the only thing hiding us from the Nazis was their own stench.

No one had to teach me to hate or fear the mud. I learned quickly enough that mud was a real enemy. Mud made walking impossible. It got into everything, and I hated its taste. Mud ruined everything. It held the cold, the wet, and the bugs. Thick mud barred us from any quick successes. Mud was the ever-present and constant threat.

The beauty of Italy did not escape me. If we hadn't been fighting, it was a place I thought I would have liked to visit or even live. It was so different from home. Cobblestone streets and old buildings were everywhere, even on the mountainside. Nothing was wild.

1943 was all war—we fought every single day and as the year deepened, so did our resolve. We were the elite and were proud of it. We fought without thinking, killed without caring, and were feared. They called us the 'Devils in Baggy Pants.'

One morning, bright and early, we moved through a tiny village that boasted only a few houses and one small church. As we moved through, I noticed movement to my right. Ever at the ready, I raised my rifle. There was no enemy, instead I noticed a small child, a girl of about seven years, watching us from the shadows of a small doorway. She had big eyes full of fear. No one else seemed to notice or care to notice her.

We continued on, but that little face haunted me. She was all alone. As I walked through her small village, I saw no other living person. We left her behind even though she was so small and vulnerable. There was nowhere to take her. I reminded myself I was a soldier responsible for killing. That was the harsh truth. We were only responsible for one duty. There was no time or energy to care for children. I was nothing more than a devil, bringing Hell across a war weary land.

By the end of December, we had dug in and were waiting for orders. As hard as we fought, the Nazis fought back just as hard. The idea we might take Rome fast and easy were sidelined and forgotten. Rome was not going to fall easily. Both sides wanted the victory, and we were nearly stalemated at Anzio.

Anzio was the Nazi's last defense, and they were going to keep it at all costs. The fight was horrifying and lasted more than four months. Nothing won that fight but sheer willpower; two American commanders were removed from duty, I thought unfairly, due to our lack of success. Most of us that enlisted resigned ourselves to the fate of painful death.

It was terrible. It was laborious gaining any ground. Each move was difficult. We gained ground, then dug in. Houses, church towers, and shops all hid our enemy if we weren't already utilizing those spaces. We, the invaders, fought against the unknown.

The streets were a mystery and the language unknown. Such obstacles only aided the enemy securing their knowledge of everything we couldn't know.

It felt more like World War One than Two. Lines were drawn, sides would be dug in behind them. Small spaces of land were won and new lines drawn, over and over again. We killed, were killed, and, finally in May 1944, we took it. That victory was so hard-won, we hardly called it a victory. There were so many dead and the 504's so depleted, we were sent to England for a short respite.

When I left home, I was young, but battle aged me. I wasn't even sure how to take respite. The Brits welcomed us alright. We drank, smoke, grabbed any girl we could, and did our best to live up to our devilish reputation. A week into the respite, I didn't feel anymore rested than the first day.

I looked around. I was surrounded by empty, stuck open eyes focusing on distant spaces. Pretty girls walked around smiling at us, but I barely registered them. I grabbed one and kissed her full on the mouth, ready to somehow end my suffering with her love. Her arms around my neck, her mouth open, I found myself clinging to her, trying to be human again. I was crying into her hair and was so afraid of letting go. She let me hold on and then stepped away. I hadn't asked her name and I didn't even watch her go. I grabbed another bottle and drank as deep as I could, praying for a release from my sins. Music played on through the night and more girls came through. Not one of us followed anyone out that night. We sat, in a row, our eyes stuck open, staring into the nothingness that had become life.

Over the next few days, I slowly began to feel human again. I stared less but I hated loud noises. Every time someone laughed too loud or shouted, I jumped. I couldn't figure it out. I was never jumpy on the battlefield. I couldn't make sense of why I was so jumpy while it was safe and quiet in England. There were no children in harm's way, and I wasn't protecting my comrades, but this was somehow worse. I relentlessly thought of so many others who were in danger. I constantly felt guilty for my hard-earned respite. Every night, I desperately tried to live.

God, I wanted to live. I wanted to drink every drop of life offered to me. I wanted to taste food, sleep until I was rested, feel every woman, and watch the sun come up every morning. I didn't want to miss out on anything. I was a soldier, though, in an unstoppable war.

We were asked to volunteer for more. We weren't told but we all guessed, the Allies were finally ready to invade France. I wanted no part.

The moment they began telling us what was needed, that horrible pinching feeling in my stomach returned with such a force, I nearly passed out. Me, a battle-hearted Devil wearing baggy pants nearly fell over. When they asked, I didn't raise my hand. We were all told it was fine, our unit was one of the hardest hit in Italy and that was why we were being given a choice. In the end, only three guys volunteered. Guilt, that would last a lifetime, washed over me as I walked away.

I had seen too much, fought too hard, and just killed too many to join. I wanted to live. After these few days off, I wanted it more than anything. I went outside to calm myself and smoke. I found a patch of mostly dry ground, something of a commodity in England,

and stood smoking and thinking. I could feel my eyes open, staring past everything.

Breathing deeply, I stood, waiting to come back. The smoke curled around my face and after a few minutes, I noticed a cat was sitting at my feet.

She was white, fluffy, and her tail bent at a strange angle. She looked up at me, with piercing blue eyes and reached her paw onto my boot. I blinked, and she was gone.

Injured

After that night, the night Rosa appeared, I felt better. I slept, peacefully, I ate, tasting the food, and I met a girl I liked kissing. My eyes weren't stuck open staring at nothing. I saw England and how green it was with all their rain. Each day, I thanked the good Lord I had somehow survived Anzio and hadn't volunteered for D-day; the three were not returning.

I knew, missing out on D-day was not going to keep me out of the war for good. I understood we would be called up again, and I was right. We spent the whole summer of 1944 in England, training. It was no vacation, but at least we weren't fighting. It didn't last long enough and I realized it could never have lasted long enough, no matter how long it had lasted. No part of me wanted back into the fight.

By August, our unit was re-supplied with new numbers and we were called up. The pinching feeling in my stomach was back. The entire unit was all glider pilots, paratroopers, or pathfinders. Most of us were at certified in more than two. We were told we were unstoppable; after all, we flew engine-less planes, dropped behind enemy lines, found our way with no maps, and killed with quiet precision. We weren't invincible but we were damn well unstoppable; we were the Devils.

After the Normandy invasion, the Allies slowly moved inland. Resistance was as tough as ever. France was still Nazi-controlled and US 504's had an impossible job ahead of us. We were briefed on rivers and their tributaries throughout France into Germany. Taking the bridges meant an early end to the war and that is all anyone talked about—the end of the war.

Nearly every conversation began or ended with, "After the war." All our dreams, all our future and past were wrapped into the end of the war. It was a terrible way to live. We were caught in a violent limbo with no promise of survival. We fought for the end of the war.

Market Garden was difficult, if not impossible. We would drop in by gliders and chutes, scattered from France to Holland. We would be scattered and possibly miles from our assigned bridge. Our unit was assigned Grave Bridge.

Each drop was planned with micro precision. They never worked out like they were planned thanks to several issues. Keeping us from precision were our battles with the elements, poor maps, emotion, and, of course, enemy fire. Most drops scattered gliders and men at least three-five miles off target and units were separated, creating an "every man for himself" situation from the moment they left the planes. It was terrifying.

The night before, we cut our hair into mohawks and painted our faces. We looked into each other's faces, admiring our warrior personas. War paint on, we were ready and willing to fight. Looking across the back of that plane, I couldn't help but admire how fearful we looked.

Surprisingly, our drop was successful. There was no bad weather and no enemy fire. We were dropped, mostly together, in sight of our bridge. Unlike most units, our personnel landed to each side of Grave Bridge. We only lost two Dakotas from our gliders, and no one was killed during the drop. We met up with some Poles and readied to take our bridge. We seized the bridge with almost no fight. Germans had destroyed two nearby bridges before we even landed. Thankfully, we were not lulled into false security. We took the bridge but we were entirely surrounded by the enemy.

A terrible fight ensued. The Allies took most of the bridges, sustaining huge losses. Each of us who survived, carried man after man on our backs up the banks of the river to safety. There were so many wounded, a short respite was called for each side to care for them. Even after D-Day, after Anzio, this was bad and because the operation was so widespread, casualties were high. I was exhausted after three days of fighting with almost no respite. I wondered how we could continue.

Leadership argued over the importance of the mission. The Brits wanted to destroy the bridges. They wanted to keep the Germans from gaining any ground that was so hard fought. The Americans wanted to keep the bridges so we could use them. We had to control the bridges to even make such a decision and in the end, we failed. The Germans destroyed the bridges.

Three and half days of hard fighting, no respite, casualties on both sides numbering in the thousands, and most disappointingly, no quick end to the war. I found myself separated from my unit, behind enemy lines with no food, no water, and really no good idea of how to join back up with my unit. I was exhausted, still encountering enemy forces with no good survival plan.

I was hungry, thirsty, and tired of being outside. All my training kept me alive but as I searched for my unit, sheer exhaustion settled in and kept me from success. Being out there on my own exasperated all my needs and terror. France was still held by the Nazis and everywhere I turned seemed more formidable. All I wanted was to eat and sleep, but the enemy was behind every tree and all. Roads were littered with land mines. I was filthy—blood, not my own, had soaked through my shirt. Each time the smell hit me, I vomited till my stomach was empty. There was no easy way out, so I kept walking.

I walked all through a black night, tripping over each rut in the road, over each stone. I ignored my rumbling stomach and dry mouth. Distant thunders ensured me I was still perilously close to danger. Out of all the nights in that war, so far, this was the worst.

I was on the edge of some damn village when the sun began its day's journey. I couldn't help but notice and truly appreciate the purple sky, the orange clouds, and the stillness unique to morning. It was quiet, and the ground began showing signs of moisture. Dewdrops hung onto each blade of grass, each branch, and each leaf. Even the distant blasting was quiet. I walked along, not seeing anyone and for at least three days, that was the last thing I remembered.

I woke, some three days later, in a large room with a hell of a headache. My head was heavily bandaged, my legs were stiff. Both my hands were wrapped. I woke with a start and immediately tried to sit up. "Non!" penetrated my foggy mind. I ignored it.

Two small hands, with clean nails, reached from the darkness and firmly pushed my shoulders back. I was too weak to really struggle and fell back against a soft pillow. I was out of breath and completely fatigued. I couldn't even ask where I was before I fell into a dark sleep lasting several more hours. The next time I woke, it was dark.

"Reste en bas, repose-toi. Ta tête a été gravement blesse." I knew enough French by then, all pathfinders did, that I understood I was hurt and should rest. My head understood this, but my heart leapt in fear inside my chest. I had no idea where I was, or how I got there. Most terrifyingly of all, I had no true idea what injuries I'd sustained or how I had gotten them. A pretty pale face, framed in dark curls, loomed over me. The soft, firm voice belonged to her. I focused all my attentions on her face.

Her eyes were wide, ringed in tired dark circles and full of concern. My vision was clearing and so was my brain fog. My head pounded, and my entire body was on fire with pain.

"Where am I? What happened?" My voice sounded off, not like me at all. It was loud, dry, and full of fear. I tried to steady it, but my throat was so dry, it cracked. "What happened to me, where am I hurt?" The pretty face looked back at me, understanding even with difference of language.

She, very softly, told me, "Shhh. Nous vous avons trouvé il y a trois jours. Vous avez marché sur une mine terrestre. Et vous avez été poignardé, ici." As she spoke, she uncovered my right leg, then my left side. As I looked down, the pain in both increased.

My brain struggled against her words, trying to understand. Mine Terrestre—that was landmine. Poignarde—that was stabbed. The words hit my heart like a dagger tearing through. I had stepped on a land mine, that is why I felt fire. My side ached, deep inside, from the stab wound. I had never felt so helpless. I couldn't tell how badly I was injured only how much pain I was in. I turned my head away from the pretty face and hair, ashamed to feel tears well up in my eyes.

There I lay, in war paint, filthy with a mohawk cut, crying. Later, I tried to figure out what exactly had brought out so much emotion. I think it was because I was afraid. I didn't know where I was; I was afraid of losing my leg. Even though she told me I'd been there for three days, I was still deeply tired.

She was a good nurse. She rubbed my shoulder and walked away. She understood I needed to be alone. I cried for a long time. I cried myself back to sleep. My slumber was punctuated with nightmares.

A tall, older man stood over me. He held a small knife in his hand. My leg was on fire, literally. I was trying to put it out with my hands, patting it, burning my hands. Simultaneously, I was busy shielding as much of my body from the threat standing over me. His head was turned over his right shoulder, and he was yelling something. Suddenly, he turned back and leaned forward. He stepped on my right arm, holding me vulnerable in front of him. I woke up.

I couldn't stop shaking even when I realized I was warm in a bed. Another pretty face leaned over me, this time it had dark eyes with light hair. She was gently rubbing something into my face and whispering, "Calme, vous êtes en sécurité. Tu es blessé mais tu es en sécurité." I noticed she said the words readily, easily. My shaking was not bothering her, nor was the fact I had called out during my sleep. She was used to this; it was just one more wound to treat.

I allowed myself to believe her. I allowed her to continue washing me and redressing my body. I didn't say a word while she was humming a song I didn't recognize. It felt nice to be treated so gently. All I had to do was focus on her low voice. My heart calmed. My stomach stopped pinching. I even got up enough courage to look over my body as she changed my bandages.

My leg was ugly, torn up from my knee to my foot. It looked as if something had torn it, lengthways, into four sections, then those four sections were each torn into innumerable parts. It was sewn up, and while it still resembled a shin and calf, there was a lot of blood oozing out. The lines of the stitches were crooked, but there were no broken bones. My foot was still attached. Even though the pain was nearly unbearable beneath the burns and stitches, I could tell it would heal. It would be ugly, but it would heal.

My hands were badly burned, probably from me patting my leg down as it burned. They also hurt, but I was assured they were mostly second-degree burns, not third or worse; they, too, would heal.

My side was badly hurt but again, I had been lucky. No major organs or any of my guts had been cut. The blade must have been small and though it went in deep, it had gone in clean and came out clean. That wound, too, would heal.

I lay back, exhausted again and asking for "eau." Another pretty nurse brought it to me and helped pour it down my throat. When I finished, she brought another. The water felt good and cold on my dry throat. I wasn't sure I would ever get enough to drink again, it felt so good.

I spent the next few days the same way. I would sleep, wake from nightmares, eat, and drink. Pretty nurses changed my bandages and helped me to the bathroom. At first, I was only let out of bed to go to the bathroom. They only let me drink water and only fed me plain broth.

Soon, those changed too though. I gained back my strength and soon, I was having as much therapy as possible. I wanted to rejoin my unit as soon as possible. The therapy was hard. The wounds slowly healed revealing new skin that was tender, easy to tear, and stiff. I hated every minute of it but I had a distraction.

Margeurite

Being injured was difficult as I expect it is for everyone. I hated not feeling well, not being able to move, the smell of the hospital, my slower movements. Most of all, I hated feeling helpless. Looking around our small ward, I realized I was not alone with my feelings, although there were a few young men that seemed at peace with this part of their life. The only thing I really liked about being injured was the fact I was injured in France with the most beautiful nurses I had ever seen.

There were five nurses assigned to each ward. Every ward was full of young men—Germans, Poles, French, American, Brits, and Aussies. It seemed like every single space was packed with me waiting to heal. Each nurse worked at least twelve-hour shifts. All the patients got to know each nurse reasonably well thanks to the long hours we spent in that facility.

I loved those nurses. I had my favorites, of course, but each one was young, beautiful, gentle, and overworked. They were aged from twenty to twenty-five and extremely dedicated to their work. Working tirelessly and efficiently, their uniforms never lost their starch, repelled stains, and even though their eyes were weary, their make-up and hair was always neat. I never could make out how they did it. Their work was demanding and difficult, yet they showed up each day, every day on time, smiling and ready to work. No matter where their patients were from, they showed them respect and demanded quiet and considerate wards. The largest nurse probably weighed in at one-thirty, but no one dared question any of them. We quieted when we were told and swearing was kept to the barest minimum. I admired those nurses—they were everything to look at, but more than that, I respected them, and every single guy in our ward also respected them, so we mostly behaved.

There was one nurse, she was short with dark auburn hair cut short. She kept it in neat curls that framed her face. She, and most of the other nurses, always used red lipstick. Her lips were full and promising. She had wide-set green eyes with long lashes. She was a quieter nurse, quick and clean with everything she did. She took care of each soldier as if he were the only one she would ever see again; she was quick but un-rushed. She asked each of us—sincerely—how we were, how we felt even though she spoke only a few words outside her own language. She was not the prettiest nurse in our ward but she was the best; my favorite. Her name was Marguerite, her name beautiful, encompassing, and even as mysterious as her.

I knew much more French than she did English, so we spoke in mostly French. Marguerite was extremely smart, and it showed in her quiet, curious manner. She took in each patient, each wound, and then proceeded to care for the patient. Many nurses would simply walk up, unwrap bandages, put new bandages on, say a few caring but rushed words, and then carry on to the next bed. They were friendly, good at their work, and extremely overwhelmed and so was Marguerite but she never showed it. One night, a particular bad night for dreams, I woke to her standing over me, holding a glass of water.

She took my bandaged hand gently in hers and gave me the water, all the while looking deep into my eyes. Even as I drank that water, she stared into my eyes. When I finished, she took a small cloth and wiped off my forehead and my face, all the while looking into my eyes. When my gaze drifted, she gently turned it back to her. After a few minutes, I noticed gold flecks in the brown of her eyes. When I stopped trembling, she put her arms around my shoulders and just held me for a few minutes. She was soft and strong; her uniform was lightly scented with laundry powder, and I felt safe. She never said a word, just took the water glass, and walked away. I watched her quietly leave the ward, her small quick steps nearly silent and barely a swing in her hips.

A few days after that night, I woke feeling more rested than I had since I was injured. I realized I had stopped suffering those terrible nightmares.

I noticed more around me. For instance, we were in a makeshift hospital. I think it was some sort of barn, and we were on the second floor. The outside walls were old and made of stone, inside it was extremely warm even though the floors were quite rough and made of wood. Our beds were cots with mattresses. The windows were blacked out with dark blankets during the night, but each morning, one nurse uncovered them, allowing the sun to penetrate even the darkest corners of the building.

There was a cafeteria on the first floor and once I was up walking, it was expected I take my meals there. I didn't mind—it was nice to have that normalcy. Wounded came in and the healed left every day. Some died, and I saw they were taken and buried in a plot dedicated to their memory. It was not far, but each burial, though quick, was done well.

Each newly dead body was gently lowered into the ground. A priest was always present and at least one nurse stood by. Often, they would move down a line of those waiting for burial. One after another, they were gently lowered, prayed over, and finally covered. I watched the ritual, each day, silently from a large doorway. I wasn't afraid. I wasn't particularly drawn to the macabre detail but I wanted to remember the many nameless who rest there.

After a week or so of watching, two things stood out. One, a few nurses, but not all, participated. The same few would almost take turns to stand, rain or sun, to bury those they had cared for, one of them was

Marguerite. And in fact, Marguerite was there much more often than anyone else. She would watch, taking in each face of the dead, then bow her head as they were put to rest. It was as if she were trying to always remember them as a person she truly cared for, instead of just another patient, just another loss. Even on her off days, she would stand at the edge of each grave, out of uniform, praying over each loss. I noticed she never brought an umbrella, never cared for her own comfort, and resolutely stayed until all were in the ground.

I had observed her duty for the dead for a few days, my attentions focused on her and her role. I saw the bodies, the priest, and the gravediggers, but most of my attention was always on her. I wondered why she chose to stand out there and how well she had known those being buried. She never spoke during or as she walked away, she simply brought a much-needed presence of meek humanity to the ritual. After a few days of watching Marguerite, I saw the cat.

I have no idea where that cat came from, if Marguerite owned her or if she simply lived near the barn. Either way, I noticed the cat also went to nearly every burial. She stood, at the edge of each freshly dug hole as if she knew what was happening. She observed each body. Her eyes would slowly blink, and she would bow at the end. Unlike Marguerite and the few other nurses, she would wait for the burial to finish before walking away.

She was small, white, and fluffy with big blue eyes. Her ears were pink and her tail bent at an odd angle. She never made a sound, I never even heard mewling at night. I never saw her anywhere else; it was as if she would appear to bury the dead. It was as if she somehow understood precious few were there to grieve, so she went in their absence.

I felt my body healing and I began to get restless during that process. The pain lessened each day, and my feelings for Marguerite deepened. When I asked her to take charge of my physical therapy, she surprised me by happily complying with no hesitation. She was tough, demanding the best of me even when my breathing and heart rate increased, sweat pouring from my face. Every day, even on Sundays, she woke me early, and we worked for two hours before breakfast.

We didn't talk while we worked. The work was too hard, and there was the language barrier. She praised my efforts and I'd compliment her, mostly in English which made her laugh. She would reply "Oui," never knowing she was agreeing to marriage.

Soon, she would breakfast with me and was telling me of her family. She was the youngest of five, the only girl. Her parents were not far and had paid for her schooling, though she never understood how they came up with the money. Before the war, before the Nazis overtook France, she had dreamt of never leaving her little village. She wanted a small home, near her mother's, where she would raise her family just as she'd grown up. Now, she wasn't sure. I'm proud to say that I could understand nearly everything she told me. I couldn't always answer but I understood. One day, I leaned across the table and I kissed her instead of answering.

Her eyes widened in surprise; her cheeks grew a little red but she never stopped telling me about the time her older brother threw her into a pond to teach her how to swim. She was pleased, I could tell even though she barely acknowledged it. After that, she touched my arm and my leg and I often saw her watching me from the corner of her eye.

As my hospital stay lengthened, so did my patience and tolerance for being there. No longer bored, I looked forward to each day knowing what to expect. Marguerite came in every day, and when she was gone, I missed her.

I tried to imagine her family. I wondered if she favored her mother or father. I wanted to meet her brothers and hear what she was like when she was little. She told me she grew up in the same house her entire life. I understood her family was not wealthy but comfortable. She grew up next door to her grandmother. She lost uncles during the Great War, and her mother still missed them. All of her cousins were involved in the war effort in some way, and Marguerite wrote to all of them. She couldn't understand some of my childhood stories but I made her laugh when I told her about our baby sister, the patate. Her eyes filled with shimmering tears when I told her about her and my father dying, and she got goose flesh when I told her about Nils and

Mama. I told her bits about Peter but left out some of his colorfulness.

She asked if the mountains in Wyoming resembled the Alps. I wasn't too sure about that. Wyoming mountains were nearly void of humans, there were no old villages on well-traversed paths. There were no mountain monasteries. Most of all, there was no war in those mountains. I missed the mountains and when I said I didn't want to talk about them anymore, she understood. She said, "Ma maison me manque aussi."

Soon, I found myself escorting her out of the hospital towards a small church ravaged by war. I knew it was empty and I felt sure Marguerite knew as well. We stepped through a bombed-out wall, careful to stay away from a leaning tower and found a bench near the back. Marguerite was quiet, holding onto me as we sat down. She kept her eyes open when I kissed her as I pulled her small body on top of mine. I saw the gold flecks and felt her tongue enter my mouth. She wasn't afraid—she wanted me as much as I did her. She unbuttoned her sweater, unashamedly exposing her undergarments and excited to share this time with me. She gently pushed me back till I was lying down and she stretched out on top of me, never breaking eye contact.

It was amazing. She was amazing. For a few precious minutes, the war was over, the world at our fingertips and our futures bright. Nothing mattered. I was whole and she loved my fresh scars. I kept her safe and happy. All too soon, we finished and helped each other dress and left that sacred space. We didn't talk all the way back to the hospital.

Marguerite left me there. I walked to my bed and sat for a time, thinking. I loved that girl, I knew. She was one in a million and I didn't care if we stayed in France or we moved to Wyoming; as long as we stayed together, my life would be complete. I couldn't help smiling.

That same day, I was released. I was healing fine, the doctor told me, I could leave and rejoin the Americans. That horrible pinching feeling was back in my stomach—I didn't want to leave.

I was told I could stay the night then join a small group who were leaving early the next morning. All I could do was wait and hope Marguerite would come back before I left. Then, we heard the bombs.

Everyone panicked. It was as if we had been living in an oasis, apart from the world and that sound brought it all back. The bombs were close—we could hear buildings collapse and we ran for cover. Thankfully, the attack only lasted a few moments. Then, the screams started.

I was safe and uninjured, so I left my small hiding place and ran back towards the hospital. It was gone— only the foundation remained. It looked like not all had gotten out and the rubble was strewn with a few body parts and blood. I looked around for survivors the best as I could. I looked back towards the place the village had been.

No one was running from there. No nurses or doctors were running around looking for new patients. There was nothing. The houses that had once occupied the few streets were gone. I knew there were no survivors and I knelt, no longer able to hold myself upwards. I couldn't understand what had even attracted the Germans to this place. It was a sleepy little place, no threat to anyone. The hospital had been set up in haste—it was no threat. The church stood no longer. As I looked across the clearing dust, I saw even the small signpost announcing the town name was gone. It was all gone.

Then, a small movement from the corner of my right eye caught my attention. That white cat was headed towards the place the hospital stood. She walked right by the old building and headed to the graveyard. She slowly walked by each new grave, then made her way back. She sat at the edge of it, looking stoically across. Instinctively, I knew she was the only survivor. I knew she would keep vigilance over this place, forever guarding the price it paid for the horribleness of war.

I turned and walked back to a gathering crowd of the few survivors. I helped gather people and supplies best as we could. We made the choice to use the barn again, at least for the night, resolving to leave in the morning with as many as we could. There was nothing left here.

Battle of the Bulge

It was time to leave. We left in pairs, in threes, and in fours, joining the river of people who were lost, looking for stable rightness in a world gone mad. I had little food and water. All I wanted was to get away from France, away from the fighting. I joined up with a couple of guys from Britain and one Pole, reasoning if we stuck together, we would be safer. We didn't talk much and no one introduced themselves. I called both the Brits 'Brit' and the Pole 'Lock.' They called me Yank. It was enough.

The autumn of 1944 was a crazy time. The days were hot and the nights cold. There was an almost constant threat of rain. I was back in that goddamned mud, and the thick tensions of war permeated me from every angle. I just wanted it to be over, one way or another. Every face I looked into was little more than a tired mask, moving along spurred by necessity of survival. Food lost its taste. My chest hair grew into the fiber of my shirt and onerously pulled with every move I made. My boots were heavy with mud. When I cleaned them off, more mud stuck to them. There was nothing to do except walk forward.

After a solid week of walking, I found myself content. I wasn't in battle and I did not miss it. I had been out of the fight for nearly two months and I began questioning if my training was still intact; I wondered if I would still be able to kill. That horrible pinching feeling settled deep into my gut and never left. The threat of returning to battle consumed my thoughts, taking away my rest and any happiness I might have found. It was exhausting.

Looking around, I saw many on the same journey. I realized how bleak life was, in that moment, those years. It didn't matter where anyone came from or how much money we had. It didn't matter what someone called their god. For those years, we were forsaken, on our own, in an earthly made Hell, abandoned of hope and faith. We were fighting the worst demon, created and inflicted by man, unleashed on all mankind. That is what truly exhausted me, stealing my essence from my very soul. There is no rest for the weary in such a world void of hope. Still, I walked.

It took nearly two weeks to reach an allied camp. My companions and I were so exhausted, all we wanted was a corner, out of the way, to find rest. Someone pointed us to the showers, then the mess hall and the four of us figured we would rest easier if we took care of ourselves. Taking my shirt off for the first time in two weeks was painful, and I tried to take my time. Once I was out of it, I removed the rest of my clothes and got into the shower.

The water wasn't warm but it wasn't cold. I let it wash over, through my hair and down my face and back. I turned towards it, allowing it to rinse my eyes and every inch of my face. The water rinsed away the grime and then some of the bleakness of the last two weeks. I washed and washed then rewashed my hair and skin. I finally stepped out into a clean but course towel, feeling better. It was only a lukewarm shower but thankfully, it had done more than clean my filthy body.

I had clean clothes to change into and then I stepped to the mirror for a shave. My hair had grown, the top too long and the sides filling in from the mohawk I had before. My beard was scraggly, long, and unkept. I looked myself over and realized I still looked like me. My eyes were still the brightest blue, and my hair was still curly and wiry. My cheeks had sunk in a little but the changes I felt so deep inside were not present on my face. I thought my eyes would have sunken into my head, mirroring my hopelessness. I was surprised and while I shaved, I checked several times to see that I was still young and still alive. Only I stared back at me.

I had left the Brits and Lock somewhere between shower and mess hall. I never saw them again. It saddened me just a little, but I wasn't surprised. It was too chaotic to hope to keep new friends. I ate a good, hot dinner alone even though I was surrounded by what felt like thousands of people. After, I slept and slept.

My dreams were filled with gold flecks, my father's one eye, and white cats guarding potatoes. The dreams didn't frighten me, but they reminded me of all I'd lost during my short twenty-three years. I woke wondering how my mother was and the last time anyone had heard from Peter.

It took a little while but I finally tracked down members from my unit. We caught each other up on the past months. Turns out, I had been injured the worst but had the best stay. Several guys met French girls and those pictures were passed around. I didn't discuss Marguerite.

We stayed on for a few more day, all the while more men showed up, looking for rest. Units went out on small missions and all of us readied for the next big push. We had no idea it would come so hard and fast. Somehow, the Germans still had plenty of fight in them.

December 1944 was cold and bleak as the autumn was. It was as if the seasons even understood how bleak the war was and played accordingly. Snow came early, much earlier than anyone expected and only added to the hardships we faced daily. A small favor came with the chill. When it froze, there was no mud. There was so much snow, even I, with my long legs, was knee deep in the drifts. It was cold, we were underfed, and no one wanted to spend another holiday in Europe ever.

We knew the Germans were up to something; they were too quiet. Thanks to the snow, we stood out like sore thumbs in our olive drabs. Some kid named Pezzone came up with the great idea to take white bed sheets from houses for camouflage. The crazy idea worked. We dropped in behind those enemy lines one night, covered in bed sheets and hidden in the snow, and hunkered down. I spread a sheet over me and my buddy in our hole and the German spotlights drifted over us time and again.

Later, I learned over two hundred thousand German soldiers were readying for an all-out offense to kick us off the European continent. Two hundred thousand, war-weary, hungry, ill-equipped Germans lined up, ready to die for their mad leader. Europe held its collective breath as stories of Nazi-savagery spread.

Stories of mass murder came in every single day. Germans were dressing as Allied soldiers, then murdering civilians indiscriminately on their march towards the Rhine River. No prisoners were taken. Christmas was bleak.

I heard from Mama, Aunt Anya, and even Peter, though his letter was old. Each letter brought my thoughts closer to home, close to the people that loved me most. I treasured them and folded each one carefully, tucking them inside my shirt. They were safe there and ready to reread anytime.

Mama's letter was the hardest to read. She talked about the weather and Nils. There was nothing of great significance, but it made me miss home. I missed her, Nils, and that neat little house we called home. I missed fishing in the creek in the back yard and the smell of autumn leaves mixed with fresh mountain air and pine trees. Anya's brought a smile to mind and face. Hers was full of gossip.

The women in the house where I grew up were still there. Now, though, they were respected members of the community. They worked as mechanics. Others worked transporting goods in big trucks. All tended a victory garden they put in behind the vast building. Kate was especially driven and was now training young women to garden and be a mechanic. I was amazed and pictured her in overalls. She would always look good; nothing could quiet cover her curves.

Peter was somewhere in the Alps, and much of his letter was blotted out; apparently, the censors didn't like his details. Towards the end, he talked about some Italian girl he was in love with. He described her long hair and large eyes, but neglected to say her name. I wondered if that was on purpose. I wondered if she was still alive.

The letters reminded me there was life beyond that war, away from the mud and cold. Winter would not last forever, and this war couldn't last forever either. All I had to do was survive.

We dug in, refusing to give any ground to the opposing tide of Nazis. After just two days of fighting, our unit was separated, and I had no idea what was happening. There was no way to know. I wondered how in the hell any of us would survive.

German soldiers dressed in stolen uniforms and infiltrated our lines. They killed randomly and viciously.

Every single day, more and more reports from the East spoke of horrific death camps. My hate for the war, for Europe, and especially those Nazis grew as the fighting grew harder. In the meantime, winter silently crept over Europe, and the cold was life threatening.

It crept into our bodies, settling deep, into our bones, exhausting us and taking over our minds. My hands were constantly stiff with it. My body constantly shifted, trying to gain some warmth. It was exhausting. I never truly rested and plenty young soldiers froze to death during the night. I feared the cold as much as I feared the Germans.

We settled in, grim but determined. Soon, it seemed the cold was stronger. It permeated every layer, every man, crawling up our coat sleeves, under our hats, and into our minds each night. We tried to keep moving, we tried to think of warmer thoughts, but after two weeks, our grim determination was lessened.

The third week, the Germans threw all they had at us. There were so many explosions and concussions, so many blasts, I nearly gave up any hope. That night, I was so exhausted, so overcome with the cold, I barely acknowledged I still lived. Surviving was all I did. I didn't feel and I didn't hope. Minute by minute, I survived.

The battle raged on for six full weeks. People gave up. You could see it in their eyes as the hope and will to survive abandoned them. They grew still, giving up on keeping warm and wouldn't even shield themselves from blasts. We found them in the mornings, eyes frozen open, staring into nothing.

Then, came the deserters far more than anyone anticipated. It was the strangest thing when they decided they no longer wanted to fight the cold and the enemy. Most just walked away. Some took more extreme measures to leave.

I saw one young man shoot his own foot. I would have let him lie, waiting for help. Unfortunately for him, I wasn't the only one who saw him. I didn't stick around to see if he was properly buried or not. Others were ordered to be shot for deserting. After six weeks, we were victorious. The other side backed down. There was still a fight, but the Battle of the Bulge had ceased.

Soon after, I heard of an ongoing operation. There was a pretty, German-born, USO entertainer working in England. She constantly asked anyone to deliver mail from her to her mother. Several soldiers carried letters back and forth for her, happy to do something so humane. They had even gotten together and secretly flown the girl to her mother. One guy described the scene.

"We flew the girl to the edge of a small German village, almost completely surrounded by thick forests. Her mother was already there, ready to meet her. It was such a touching reunion, not one of us battle-hardened soldier kept their dry eyes. The girl ran to her mother and never let her go as long as she was there. The two conversed for nearly an hour in their native tongue and the mom often touched her daughter's hair and cheeks.

The girl begged her mama to go with her, to board the plane and fly to safety. The mother gently refused. She would stay back and care for her own mother who was physically unable to care for herself. The pretty young girl begged her, tears ruining her mascara but her mother refused. Then, the girl decided to stay; she did not want to leave her mother. Her mother refused this too. She handed her over to us. I caught the young girl and led her away from her mother. I think we all knew this was the last time they would see each other, and it damned near broke all of us. I led her back to her plane and helped her sit safe inside. She turned and waved to her mother, crying too hard to call anything out." His voice broke at that. He took a few seconds to take a long drag from a cigarette, then he told me the rest.

"Her mother, squared her own shoulders and waved back, even managing to smile before we closed the door. Two soldiers led her away, through the dark, safe to her own home." I was astounded at these events and before I knew it, two weeks went by, and I found myself at the service of that young girl. Her mother was killed by a blast to her neighbor's home. The concussion had caused her own roof to fall in, killing both her and her invalid mother while they slept. The girl asked for us to bury her mother but we did more than that.

Again, she was hidden on a plane and flown to that same village. During the darkest time of night, she was taken to the old cemetery where she was reunited with her mother for the last time. Here, I put my arm around her small shoulders and led her to the place we had readied for her mother's body. I stood beside her while they lowered the body into the ground. The girl wept, almost silently, and I stood there wishing to God I could take her pain away. We stood there while they buried her. When they finished, she dropped to her knees, panicked, whispering, "Mama, Mama!" over and over again in a hoarse, raw voice. We finally got a hold of her and dragged her away. I don't think she would have left, ever, had we not done that for her. We got her on the plane and she flew away.

"I lost many people early in my life but witnessing this woman bury her mama hurt. I was reminded of home, of the possibilities of the future, and what true love meant. I still faced the cold, I still faced the Germans, but this gave me a reason to fight, a reason to live. While I walked away, I wondered how anyone could survive such a god-awful place."

Still Fighting

I was tired—tired of the cold, tired of fighting, tired of hating, and tired of the army. I was tired of war. I wanted to go home. Home.

When I thought of home, my mind took me to a happy place. There were no lines waiting for food, waiting to jump or waiting to shower. Home was warm. Home had happy people waiting to see me, to feed me. They were happy to see me. It became unbearable to live apart from home. I realized nothing could ever replace it and living in cold mud sure as hell didn't help.

War was my reality, though. My days were spent fighting and waiting in lines. On good days, I waited for my turn to eat, to shower and to sleep. I was stuck in Europe. It was a strange place and time. Europe was old, and nothing was sacred. They bombed their old buildings and churches simultaneously killing off their own population and history. War destroyed it all. Everywhere I looked, more and more people were displaced, and more and more homes were wrecked beyond repair.

I was stuck in a place I did not want to be and I was miserable. I wanted to leave Europe; I wanted the war over. The early months of 1945 were the worst.

I had already survived so much. I was still alive after enduring terrible injury. The greatest, longest battles hadn't killed me. I survived four drops. I survived being lost and separated from my unit. I was a lucky one. I had all my limbs. I had my life. I told myself how lucky I was, but I missed Marguerite and all my friends lying in cold holes. I missed the sun and warm garden in my mother's home. I missed my brother.

I had no contact with Peter for months and there was no way to know if he was another lucky one. Day to day life was simple survival, and no way for anyone to truly live.

Between the mud and the cold, we were still clearing Nazis. Thankfully, the fighting was not as intense but there were daily fights. We killed so many. I killed so many. I was so consumed by my own survival that it took a while to notice the enemy had changed.

Germany was losing the war. It became increasing evident as March approached. One day, not unusually, I found myself on the receiving end of enemy fire. I was holed up in a bombed-out building with only half the walls intact. I was half-asleep, cold and thirsty, when I first heard the shots. They were close. I crawled to a point where I could look out.

At first, I was confused. I didn't see any shooter; all I could see was a kid. He was standing in the rain, a weapon raised in my direction. He was too young to fight, too young to be a soldier. I looked around to find where the enemy was. No one else was around. The street was empty.

I watched him, finally realizing that kid was my enemy. He was so young, too short, weighing just above a hundred pounds. I watched him for a moment. He was completely wet, head to foot. His boots looked too large and were heavy with mud. His weapon was shaking so much I doubted he could hit me. His eyes were huge with fear. I could see he was suffering from cold and hunger.

It had been months since I had allowed myself to see enemies as human. I wondered if and how many other children I had fought. Had I killed children? I desperately tried to squash those thoughts, but they poured in as I watched that poor kid. I realized I didn't want to kill him. He was on the wrong side—he was shooting at me, but he was too young for this hell. I made up my mind to help that kid. I was not going to murder him.

I never liked killing but, when faced with death, I did what I had to do. Most of the time, I just didn't have a choice—it was kill or be killed. That was war. This was different as I felt I had a choice. I could sneak out the side of my building, shielding myself until I was nearly on top of him. I doubted he would watch for me in the streets as he was too focused on my hiding place. I removed my helmet, laying it carefully in his sight, and then backed away.

I reached him in a few seconds. He saw me at the last second, his face full of terror. I simply took the weapon from his hands. I didn't even have to hit him. Then, I dragged him from the street back into my hiding place and sat him down in front of me. He swore, in German, then in English. I ignored him. He swore again. I ignored him again.

The night before, I had scavenged some food from a cupboard in the house. There wasn't much and I wasn't too sure where it came from or how long it had been there but I was beyond caring. I took out one can. I was hungry. I could tell the boy was too. He stopped his swearing and watched what I was doing. His mouth slightly opened and a trickle of drool escaped from the right corner. I took notice; I had been right that he was hungry. I took my time offering him anything. I carefully took a couple of bites from the can of food and then looked up at him. Another trickle escaped from his mouth. I made him wait.

After a full three minutes, I handed him the can. He didn't even take the spoon I offered. He just took the can, tipped it to his mouth, and ate the entire contents in a matter of seconds. I was already opening the next. He took that one as well and ate it all. Then, he closed his eyes and leaned back, falling asleep in what seemed like a matter of seconds. On closer inspection, I noticed dark circles beneath both eyes and wondered how long he'd been awake.

I never said a word, I just let him sleep. He reminded me of me when I was his age. That realization woke something deep inside me. Here was this kid who should have been in school, studying and making friends but was out shooting at men. I hated Hitler more than ever. He stole so much from so many.

Every day, we heard rumors of death camps and of the Jews he was murdering. Every day, we saw more and more people displaced and fatigued by a war that had no end in sight. I glanced outside; it was raining again which meant more mud, more cold, more dampness. Even the skies seemed like they were against us.

I let the kid sleep. I couldn't believe it when he slept for solid four hours. When he woke, he asked for more food and water, which I readily gave. I didn't really know what to do with him. I didn't really want to just let him go, especially with no weapon. And I wasn't about to give it back, either. It was time for me to move, so I just took him with me.

When we made it back to the line, I took him to the fenced off portion meant for prisoners. I was hoping some of the older German men would take care of their own. It felt wrong like I was abandoning him. He couldn't stay with me, and I could never trust him. I didn't want to end up killing him. As they pushed him behind the gate, he looked back at me, gratitude in his face. I never saw him again.

After that kid, I began noticing the world again. I noticed most of the villages we came across held more life than only war. People were helping each other. It was not only me; the entire European continent was tired. We all wanted that damn war to end.

As spring hit, I noticed the leaves and new blooms. I was happy to note that Hitler, who had caused so much pain and stole so much, could not stop the earth. Slowly, I began to hope again.

I hoped for the end of the war. I hoped to see my brother again. Through my hope, I began planning my life after the war. I wanted to meet a girl. I wanted to study and find a good job. I wanted to fish again. Spring brought me so much hope, but the war still raged on. I knew we had to take Berlin to end it.

As we marched towards our final target, the Russians were marching towards us. I was excited and confused. I wasn't even sure what the end could mean after spending so long fighting. What would happen? Would we all just go home, leaving Europe to rebuild? Would it truly end? Or would it end for a few years and some mad man will start it all again? Alarmingly, I wondered how I could leave this life. *How could I stop soldiering?*

The war changed me and not for the better. Kill or be killed, survive or die. I no longer felt I was Jurak. I had no idea who Jurak was. Now, I was a paratrooper, a pathfinder, and a killer. I learned food was meant to sustain. I couldn't remember the last time I had actually enjoyed a meal. I was a soldier through and through, weary of war but no other way to live. There was nothing I could do about such fears; after all, the war was still on. The war had to end. We had to end it.

Our last target was Berlin. We knew taking Berlin would mean winning the war. We all understood killing Hitler was the only way to end it; if he lived, so would the war. Most of us talked about taking him out. Everyone wanted a quick end.

As we continued deeper into Germany, we heard more and more stories of Hitler's evil. Killing camps had killed thousands. Maybe even hundreds of thousands. As Germany ran out of young capable men to soldier, Hitler had pressed boys as young as fourteen into service and men well into their sixties into the hardships of soldiering. Young women were brainwashed to believe they were the mothers of the beginning of the greatest generation for Germany. They lined up to conceive, growing babies to be given over for state rearing. It was unthinkable, unimaginable what Germans did in the name of Hitler.

I thought back to my happy place, my home near the mountains. I could not imagine any one of my neighbors, cousins or anyone else resorting to the rumors we were hearing of what the simple German families were resorting to. It was all so criminal. They robbed people blind of any freedom, even the rights to raise their own children. It was chilling to witness how quickly Hitler turned German tradition and pride into such shit. There was no other name for it. His philosophies and his goals were all shit.

I hated him. I hated his war machine. I hated the Germans that bought into his shitty ideals and fueled his machine for war. I wondered if I would ever stop feeling that hate. Somehow, I hoped I would.

Hitler took life from all of us, though. He stole some of the best years of my life. He called me up to train, lose sleep, stand in never-ending lines, to fight, and to kill. He stole the same from numerous others and to what end? I couldn't answer those questions—no one could and none of us were ever able to.

Weary, hungry, and thirsty, we finally marched into Berlin. The Russians were there, our supposed allies. Sometimes, we stopped them stealing and raping. Mostly, though, we could not. The same rumors went around about us, and we could not deny the violence we invoked on our enemies. No one was innocent, but the Russians seemed worse, at least to me.

Berlin was quiet for an invasion. It was so bombed, so destroyed, we could only help. Everywhere we looked, there was destruction. I was amazed to see as many people as we did. I had no idea how anyone could have survived. After a few days, we heard the news.

Hitler was dead. The war in Europe was over.

A Dare to Hope

The war was over.

I, alongside the entire world, had hoped for this longer and harder than anything else. I spent *years* hoping for this, beginning almost as soon as I disembarked the bus in North Carolina to begin training three years ago, nearly down to the day I had hoped for the war to end. We heard about all the celebrations throughout the U.S., in Paris, and London. Even in bombed-out Berlin, people celebrated, though I think it was done more quietly. Men and women wiped away tears from tired faces. Everyone was weary of fighting. That first night, a kid named Smith found alcohol from God knows where, and we toasted our survival.

The first went down smooth. The second and third followed. We drank to the brothers we lost. We drank to those who died. We drank to those who would never be found. We drank to Hitler's death. I woke up, holding onto the earth for dear life, sick as I ever was, wondering why I had drunk so much. The next night, we did it again—and the night after that and the night after that. It was a wonder any of us survived the drinking.

The war *was* over, at least in Europe. We had plenty to do to keep us from worrying about fighting in Japan. Rumors swirled around. Some believed we would only help rebuild for a week or two, then ship out to Japan. Most of us wondered how the war in Japan could end without the Devils' support. I didn't want to go.

I never missed the fighting. I sure as hell didn't miss the killing. My entire adult life I had been a soldier and even though I had no idea what I was going to do when I got home, I knew I was done with soldiering. I hoped Uncle Sam would understand. I hoped and prayed the Devils would stay out of Japan.

As June seeped into July, I began wondering how long we would have to stay in Europe. There was so much to do after the war. Everywhere I looked, there was destruction. Bombed-out buildings needed new roofs. Piles of debris needed to be removed. Whole villages had been reduced to rubble. There was so much debris, I thought it remarkable anything was left standing in Europe. Besides the damaged roads and buildings, there was the mess of the people.

People from everywhere showed up, all day, every day. They wanted to get as far west as they could, no matter where their homeland was. Germany was divided in half and from what I could tell, most folks weren't too keen on becoming Russian.

We dealt with growing numbers of displaced people. Every. Single. Day. It was nearly as exhausting as the fighting, and I noticed my empathy lessened, just as it had with killing, while dealing with them.

They were a sore lot, to be honest. It was horrible seeing how little they had. Most had the clothes on their backs. Many wore mismatched shoes, others wore one. A few had blankets and small suitcases. No one had food. We set Red Cross supplies and all those people joined line after line, waiting for food, showers, or shelter. It was beyond pitiful. They all had questions with no answers. Desperate mothers asked after missing children who were surely dead. Desperate husbands called out for wives. One day, I saw a man, aged by war, stand up and run in circles shouting the name, "Freida!" over and over again. We caught him, wrapped him in a blanket, and led him to a med tent. I wondered if he could ever recover. I wondered who Frieda was.

Many Germans were happy to begin rebuilding. After all, most didn't have jobs or homes; the sooner they rebuilt, the sooner they could get on with life. Many displaced persons took rebuilding efforts with no direct orders. It was good to see the coordinated efforts, but I wasn't too sure Germany could every fully recover. All were affected, and I could tell some were lost forever.

They would sit, at the edge of a street, eyes stuck open staring into nothing. A few lucky ones had loved ones around them, caring for them. They would fetch them food and drink or wrap blankets around their thin shoulders. Still, they would sit, unable to forget whatever horrors they witnessed. I thought they were the worse of the shell-shocked citizens. Then, came a busload of Jews.

Of course, all of us heard about the Jews. It was different seeing them. Even though they should be up several weeks after their liberation, many still looked like walking skeletons. They had no belongings. When they talked, I saw many gaps where teeth should have been. Everyone, man or woman, had short hair. Not one was with a blood relation. Most of them stared, their eyes stuck open. They had nothing. They didn't even have debris to clear. Hitler stole everything from them. They huddled together still afraid to leave each other. As I watched them line up for food, I knew I would never get that awful sight out of my head, and I never did.

After a few days, the Jews left and I found myself hoping more than ever that I would stay the hell away from Japan. If Germans did this to their own people, what could Japan have done? I didn't want to find out. That second week of July hit with all the heat of summertime, and we were called up.

None of us were surprised. US Devils had played too important of a role in liberating Germany from those damned Nazis. All of us seriously doubted the Allied forces could sustain much of a fight without us. So, when the captain called us altogether, I knew what was coming.

"Those Japs are dug deep, guys. I know we fought hard here and we won, but the war isn't over yet. Get your things, we fly out in a few hours. After we get back to England, we'll board a ship to the East." The captain didn't sound excited. He didn't rally us all together with a good fighting speech. He was resigned to his fate and as I looked around, I realized we all felt the same. No one spoke as we walked away.

My heart sank at his words and it sank even further as I walked back to my bunk. I didn't want to leave Europe for Japan. I didn't want to sit my ass on some filthy ship as it sailed two oceans across the world to get me into another fight. I didn't want to go.

I sank down on my bunk, content to sit for a few minutes. I wondered why I had survived so long and so hard a fight, just to be sent off to an even worse situation. At least Europe didn't have malaria. I had heard some awful stories from Japan. I wondered if I was in good enough shape to survive Japan. I couldn't resolve my mood to lift. I felt my eyes open and stare across the room. I wondered where Peter was, if their unit was going to Japan too.

I got up and packed my few possessions, all military related. Uniforms, check. Weapon, check. Boots, check. Irrationally, I felt like bawling. I almost felt as if I were leaving home again. As I took the last steps towards the door, I realized I lived here, in this room, for over five weeks. That was the longest I had lived anywhere since jump school. I couldn't look back.

I lined up and boarded a plane. The engines drowned out any talking, and I took my place without saying anything to anyone, keeping my head down. It was too heavy a burden to look up. I felt the plane turn onto the runway and heard the rise of the landing gear. We rose into the air. I hated every minute of it. I knew I had used up all my chances on European soil. I would never make it out of Japan alive.

The flight was short. We made it to England in just a few hours and after we touched down, we were briefed on the new plan. A ship was waiting to get us all on board hopefully, the next morning, but most likely the day after that. Knowing the military by then, I figured we had two nights in England. I was right.

The boys and I lived it up. We were told to stay on base—an order we all ignored. I figured I had weeks, not months, to live and I was going to live. I drank and held onto some British girl with bad teeth, but nice hair. I vaguely remember thinking her waist was awfully thick and her accent slightly annoying when she climbed on me.

So much for really living it up. I woke up the next day in some back alley, covered in vomit I was sure wasn't my own. My head pounded and the little bit of sun filtering through the English gloomy sky penetrated my aching eyes. Once again, I resolved drinking was no way to live and walked back to the base. Once there, I literally thanked the good Lord out loud, being right the day before. They weren't ready for us to board the ship. I slunk back to my bunk and laid down without washing. I slept well into the evening until Smith woke me up with, "I figure we have weeks, not months. Let's go live."

I showered and met him at the gate. I repeated the night before but this time, I made it back to the base and collapsed on my bunk. I could never recall how I got there.

The next day, we lined up with our aching heads and all our gear, ready to board. The water did not help my side effects of living. It was long before I found myself lined up against the rails, vomiting. I resolved never to drink again.

Two days into our voyage, and fully recovered, I kept to my resolution. I ate well and kept up my exercising, running laps around the deck. I figured the best way to survive the Japs was to gain as much muscle as I possibly could while I could. It felt good taking such a stand. I began to hope I could survive another war. After three days at sea, we turned back to collect another unit. We didn't even get to leave the ship, we stayed in dock a couple of days, more people boarded, and we turned into the sea again.

July was well over by then, and I could feel August even though I hadn't been keeping too good a track of the actual days. We were a little more than halfway to the United States when we got the news. Japan had surrendered.

I survived the war.

That night, we were given two beers with dinner and I relished them with gusto. I pawned another off a devoutly religious man and relished his. I almost couldn't believe I survived the war.

That thought kept me up all night, and I watched the sunrise. I survived the war. I was no longer a soldier. I survived the war. Tears ran down my face. I stayed at the rail of that ship, watching the sky turn its glorious shades of pinks and oranges, and I prayed.

I began by thanking God for my life. I asked Him to keep all those who had died safe with him. My shoulders shook when I begged His forgiveness. I thanked Him for his Son. At the very end, even with all my gratitude, I couldn't resist asking Him why so many had to die. I closed after I asked Him why I had to kill. My tears ran dry, and I watched the horizon for a long time but I never heard an answer. As far and as long as I watched that horizon, I never understood why such a senseless war had been fought. There were so many lives stopped and so much loss endured. No voice, from the darkness or light, ever answered my question.

We pulled into New York City and were welcomed home as heroes. Our uniforms were laundered and pressed almost as soon as we disembarked. We were marching in a parade in just three days. What a spectacle.

Crowds waving, with all the women tearing up. We were offered drinks everywhere we went. I was sure glad I had resolved to live. Pretty girls in pretty dresses were waiting everywhere. Every single bar I went into, I was welcomed, slapped on the back, and asked to share my stories. I hardly got a word in edgewise. My pants were tucked into my boots and that's all people needed; they knew I was a Devil and they were proud to have me there. I never told them about the mud or killing young men handsomer and smarter than myself. And I never told anyone about Marguerite. I just drank.

I was lucky. Since we were already back on U.S. soil, there was no way, we would be sent anywhere else. We weren't going back to Europe. It was too costly. I was sent back to North Carolina to out-process. I was told once I completed that, I could go home. My mind couldn't fully process the idea of going home, not while I was headed back to that backwards hot south. We lined up, again, back in Fayetteville, at good ol' Bragg, and after just a week or so, I was dismissed from the Army Corps. After three years of fighting, I was finally headed home.

All I would think about were the granite-topped mountains I had so missed. I could almost feel that wind on my face filled with the scent of wild sage. I was ready to drop my line into those fishing holes I knew so well, catch some dinner, and fall asleep on those banks. I missed Wyoming.

The bus ride would take three days and two nights to get from Raleigh, North Carolina to Denver, Colorado. I was so close, I couldn't sleep. Every stop, I was slapped on the back and welcomed home. I never bought any food or drinks. I was their hero.

Normally, I would have protested such treatment. The truth was, I wasn't sure what I was going to do with myself or how to start again and saving the cash seemed a good idea. Every now and then, I realized how lucky I was and was happy I had resolved to really live.

The only time the trip grew long was through Kansas. That land is the flattest land I still have ever seen. We drove north for hours, then made a hard left and drove more hours. It was mind numbing and most of us passengers slept. I woke up to cheers. The Rockies stood before us.

The bus then made a hard right and headed north, the Rockies to my left. My ears protested the altitude, plugging and popping. Home was so close. We pulled into another stop and I stepped off into the wind. I knew we were just outside of Denver and every ounce of me vibrated with the excitement of my new reality, my new lease on life. I took about five steps and stopped dead in my tracks. I could not believe my eyes.

There, in front of me, was my brother. Peter was passed out on the bench in front of the stop, obviously waiting for the same bus I was on. He was dead to the world, head back, mouth open, really sleeping. I noticed he had a cane there beside him on the bench but I didn't care. I hadn't seen my brother in nearly four years. I dropped my stuff and ran to him. I nearly picked him right up, and he pushed at me till he saw who I was. Peter and I had grown up together, and I couldn't recall too many times I had seen him cry. He was crying now, though. Tears ran down his cheeks, and he couldn't catch his breath. I let him down and we hugged hard, slapping each other across the back again and again. He finally pulled back and looked me up and down.

"I got three, maybe four of your letters during the entire last year. I had no idea when I would see you! You look well, Jurak. You look well." He grabbed his cane, leaned across it, and slapped my back again.

"Ahh, Peter, I haven't had any letters for the last half year, at least. I was afraid they shipped you off to Japan after we finished Europe." I didn't mention how truly afraid I was that he might have been dead in the mountains in Italy. I opened up my carton of smokes and offered him one. We sat and smoked, waiting for our bus home. We caught our next bus and sat together over that Wyoming border into Cheyenne. The bus promptly overheated, and all the passengers were encouraged to seek entertainment the rest of the afternoon. Peter and I headed to the nearest bar where we were immediately pulled in and offered drinks.

Our bus was scheduled to pull out later that night, but we missed it. Another bus came through the next afternoon and we missed that one too. Peter had always liked drinking and I could tell the war hadn't changed that. We were young, mostly fit, and the girls kept telling us how good looking we were. It was good to be home.

We spent another night and another day at that bar. I lost track of my brother, but a good guy threw my drunk, hungover ass on the bus on that third day. I collapsed onto the only open seat next to the prettiest girl I ever saw.

She was at least a foot shorter than I and had bright piercing blue eyes. Her hair was short and dark. Instinctively, I knew she was a nurse. She was sitting with her back straight, eyes forward, and chin up. She was all no-nonsense and expected the best from those near her. She hardly glanced my way even though I must have knocked into her when I tried to sit. I looked at her again, really seeing her profile.

Her nose ever so slightly turned up at the end and though she was slim her cheeks were full. Her hair was short, full, and curly at the bottom. Her lips were perfectly heart shaped and pale pink. Her skin was fair. My speech was slurred when I asked her name. To her credit, she ignored me.

A Long Ride Too Short

That bus ride changed my life. Some might judge me, saying I shouldn't have spent three days drinking, but it worked for me though. That nurse sitting next to me was worth it. I would never have met another woman half her worth had I taken a different bus.

Two hours into our trip, I woke up and realized she was still sitting next to me. Thinking I would be clever and show off my language skills, I asked her name in German. "Schönes Mädchen, Sag mir, wie du heißt." She looked at me, straight in the eye, lifting her lefty eyebrow slightly.

She held my gaze and quietly answered in flawless German, "Nein. Dein Deutsch ist schrecklich." Then, she looked out her window.

I whispered, "I don't think my German is *that* terrible. After all, I won the war speaking it."

She ignored me for a few miles, and I really panicked. I began noticing how bad I smelled and the many creases in my uniform. What had I been thinking, trying to talk to her? There she sat poised and perfect, obviously too smart, too good for the likes of me. I was feeling pretty low, when I noticed the window's reflection. She was smiling.

"Tu es la plus belle fille que j'ai jamais vue." French was the language of love, after all. And I meant what I said—she really was the most beautiful person I had ever seen.

"Dein Französisch ist schlechter als dein Deutsch." She was probably right with that; my French was pretty bad. I wondered how she knew German.

"How do you know German?" I asked. I realized I was curious about her—why she was a nurse, where she lived, and just about a hundred more questions entered my mind.

"My parents are German-born," she told me defiantly. "They moved here soon after the First World War and had us kids. They farm now." I watched her as she spoke, it must have been difficult to have German-born parents during this war.

"My parents immigrated from the Poland-Austria border; before that war, my dad was a miner. My mother still speaks to us in Polish and Czeck. Mama never liked that her country was taken from her. She wasn't born in Poland, she would tell us. She was born in Austria, and someone changed it. Her town was beautiful, in the mountains untouched by war."

I told her all about Mama then, how she married Nils and had her garden. I told her about my brother. I explained how we were separated at that bar in Cheyenne, and I had no idea where he was now. She listened, intently, and then nodded her head towards the back of the bus. I swiveled around.

Peter was there, on his own seat, asleep. "They brought him the same time they brought you. I figured you were brothers. You have the same look." Happy as I was to have found Peter again, I was even happier by the realization she had looked me over enough to see my brother and I resembled each other.

I asked her about her family, and we talked the entire way to Casper. The bus pulled into a little stop and the driver jumped out. I was afraid we would split up, but she told me she was headed north. I ran off that bus into the restroom and looked at myself in the mirror.

I was in worse shape than I thought. My uniform was badly stained on both arms and down the left side. My eyes were red, hair disheveled. My pants were untidily untucked and bunched oddly around my ankles. I had thought ahead, though, and brought my suitcase along. I pulled out a clean shirt and necessities. I brushed my teeth and hair. I took a towel and cleaned off my back and chest and under my arms. I think I smelled better when I confidently re-boarded the bus and I certainly looked better. My eyes briefly swept the back of the bus. Peter was still there, sleeping off those three days. I moved on to my own seat, but to my horror, my seat was taken.

Some good-looking bastard had stolen my seat. He was smiling at her with perfect teeth, asking her name. She smiled at him but glanced up at me. She raised her left eyebrow slightly but nodded at his words.

His hair was shiny and black, his uniform clean and pressed. Finally, he realized my presence, he glanced up.

I didn't waste any time. "You took my seat. I want it back." I watched him, keeping my gaze even and intent. I put one hand, heavy, onto his right shoulder and widened my stance.

"Funny, she never said you were sitting here," he gestured towards Inna.

"*She* has a name, and I have a seat. Move on." For the first time, he lost his smile and easy manner. I felt someone step up behind me, and I worried I might be kicked off.

"You heard him, move. That's his seat." Thank the Lord! It was Peter, not the driver, who had stepped up behind me. We stood, shoulder to shoulder waiting for the guy to move. Inna was quiet, her hands folded into her lap.

"Well, I can tell when I'm not wanted. I'll just find another seat; it was nice talking to you, and if you want to continue our conversation, I invite you to follow me." He smiled at her again. "Unless of course, you object me moving?" She looked up at all three of us, then shook her head side to side. She didn't mind him moving.

He looked a bit down but he moved on. I heard him swear under his breath as he made his way to the back of the bus. Peter slapped me on the back and took the seat across from me.

I couldn't believe my luck—I still had my seat! She had seen me at my worse and still wanted to sit next to me. I was feeling pretty good about life as I sat down. We picked up our conversation easily.

She told me about her family's farm, located in North Dakota. It sounded awful. There were no mountains and she said it was dry. Honestly, it didn't sound like a good place for a farm. I told her about the mountains. She told me about her four older brothers. Peter snored loudly.

The bus ride lasted three more hours, and I was convinced I had found my girl. The universe had pushed us together. The closer we drew to Sheridan, the more aware I became I was going to lose her.

We pulled into Sheridan, and my heart jumped. I was home. The town had changed. The trolley car was gone, but the big white building was still there. It seemed less busy, somehow. Was it me that had changed? Or had Sheridan lost that many to the war? I wasn't sure. The bus pulled into its stop, and I readied to get off. Inna watched me. I couldn't tell what she was thinking.

My heart was torn. Here I was, home. I had been hoping for nothing more for years. I wanted to see Mama and go fishing. I could never have predicted meeting Inna and now I had to leave her. I didn't move.

Peter leaned over, "Jurak, get your things; this is us." His voice was gentle but direct. He nodded to her and got off the bus. I stood up and felt my heart nearly break. I didn't want to go.

I had lost so much in life. My sister, my father, and countless friends all had been called away by some higher power. I didn't want to lose Inna. I didn't know how to make my feet take me off that bus. My training kicked in though, I grabbed my cover and made to leave the bus. My hands full, I leaned down and disembarked. I stopped to look back, wondering how in the hell I would ever find her again. Something small and soft stopped me in my tracks.

I was so overcome with my own emotion that I hadn't realized she followed me. She pressed a small card into my hand and raised up on her toes. She kissed my right cheek and climbed back onto that bus. She was so short that she didn't have to lean down at all. She stood for a moment, perfectly framed in that small doorway, and raised her hand in farewell. Her neat little suit and hat perfectly straight, her perfect smile all etched into my memory. I watched for a few minutes; I didn't want to look away. She finally turned to her own seat and the bus pulled away. I tucked the card into my shirt pocket without looking at it.

I turned towards the town. I should be grateful. I was home and that is all I had asked. I hadn't asked for the perfect girl on the bus ride there. All I had asked for was home and here I was, so I pointed my feet towards Mama and Nils' and followed my brother through those old familiar streets.

Home

As I walked up my home street, I couldn't keep my eyes away from my home. It all seemed unchanged, at least from the street. The plants and trees surrounding the garden and house were all bigger but the house was still neat in its little square yard. Enough years had gone by, I could now see trees peeking over the roof. I liked them. I liked the smell of the street and how clean it all was. I checked the rest of the street. There were no destroyed homes, no rubble and debris, and best of all, no lines of those in desperate need. This neighborhood was untouched, unscathed by the war. It was difficult to believe my own eyes.

I was home and scarred, and this haven was even more beautiful than I recalled. It was peaceful. There were no loud noises, no voices directing people towards aid or shelter. There were no alarms. I was not dreaming or wishing; I was here, I was finally home.

And there, standing at the front door, was Mama. She looked the same too. My throat constricted at the sight of her. I wanted to drop everything and run to her but I contained myself. I followed Peter, he was a bit slower with his cane, and we went up the walk together. Both of us wore our uniforms, both fighting back tears. Mama held the door wide open.

I stepped through the door. Finally, I was hugging Mama who kissed and kissed both of our faces. She laughed and cried, and so did I. I couldn't tell if Peter was or not but I felt how hard he hugged Mama. The house smelled so good, like her cooking and the soap she used for laundry. The floors were polished and not one thing out of place. I heard the backdoor open and close and heard Nils' shout.

"They home, Kat? They make it inside okay?" He came around the corner with a huge smile on his face. "I guess we can finally celebrate; the war is over, boys!"

He came across the room and hugged both Peter and I fiercely, slapped us on the back, and told Peter how bad he smelled.

"Why don't you guys clean up and then we can have dinner?" I didn't mind being dismissed. I crossed the house to the stairs and climbed up to my room. Peter, with his cane, followed.

Mama had left our room exactly the way we had left it. The beds were neatly made, the curtains pulled back, and all of it was clean. I put my bag on my bed and sat down, waiting for Peter to enter in behind me.

"I can't believe we are home." My voice was quiet, and I realized how tired I was. I told Peter to go ahead and take his shower, I didn't mind waiting.

Slumber came easily. No one woke me, there were no alarms and no shouting. For the first time in years, I woke, on my own, a few hours later. I felt rested. My mind was quiet. I got my few things together and went to take a shower.

"Maybe it is in the air," I mused quietly. I could hear noise from the kitchen downstairs and the smell of Mama's dinner wafted up, hurrying me along. As I combed my hair, my stomach rumbled at that growing smell of dinner.

I hurried down the stairs, seeing only Mama and Nils at the table. "Peter went out." Nils never sounded angry, but I could tell he wasn't pleased that Peter had left. Mama didn't say anything about Peter's absence.

We ate and drank till we were full. Aunt Anya came over soon after we finished and kissed and hugged me, and I realized why Peter had left. I was getting uncomfortable with all the attention too. Still, I didn't want to leave. I wanted to hear all the news from home. Mama talked deep into the night. She told me how most of the boys our age in our neighborhood were still away. She winked at me and told me that Miss Kate was still in town. She owned the house now.

It sounded like the war had been good to Miss Kate. She organized aid and supplies throughout Sheridan and was eventually recognized for her war efforts. She bought several plots of land and converted them into Victory Gardens. She held classes for gardening every weekend from June through September. Mama told me that Miss Kate asked about Peter and me often.

I let Mama and Nils talk, and, thankfully, they didn't ask too much about the war. I felt they just knew better. They understood, without me having to say it, that I was done with war. I wanted more from life and to leave those years behind me. Mama and Nils never pried. At that time, I thought it was for the best.

Mama did mention several boys who would never come home. I found out I lost a good friend who had grown up just a few doors down. His name was Michael, but we all called him Mike. He was strong even though he was small. He always joked and always said he would get the prettiest girl in the end. His loss was difficult to accept.

I finally went to bed. Mama let me sleep in late. She had breakfast all prepared when I came down. I hadn't seen Peter in his bed and figured he had stayed out all night. I wondered what Mama and Nils would think about that. Mama asked for my wash almost as soon as my plate was cleared. I lumbered back up the stairs, taking my time, head free from worry.

I grabbed that dirty uniform I had worn all day yesterday and removed the ribbon rack, the pins, and my belt. I went through the pants pockets. I unbuttoned all the buttons and went through the shirt pockets. Then, I felt it and remembered.

Inna had slipped me that card, and I stored it in my shirt pocket. Only her name and address were recorded on it. She was in some small town in North Dakota. I knew where to find her.

I put the card down, then picked it up. Her writing resembled her. It was even and neat, void of frills. I put the card down again.

I needed to get to her. I needed to get to North Dakota. First, I needed to work to pay for that. If I was going out there, I needed a ring. I needed some plan to live if I was going to marry her.

I brought the wash down and thanked Mama. Then, I left the house. Nils must have been at work because I didn't see him anywhere. I walked down the path towards the creek. I grabbed my fishing pole and found all my old spots. Before long, I had six good-sized fish. I cleaned them and brought them back to the house. I knew Mama would like that. I dropped the catch off in the kitchen sink and walked out the front door. I knew where to go to find work.

Miss Kate had aged and not well. She was still beautiful, she always would be, but her skin was folded and creased. She was too thin. Her hair had lost all its shine. She held her arms opened wide and kissed my cheek. I turned as she went for my mouth.

"I saw Peter last night and asked if you were home too. How are you, Jurak?" She stood with her arms folded, grinning up at me. She couldn't wait for me to answer; she was excited to tell me her own news. "I don't think I'll move to the ocean anymore. I've been workin' here while you was out fightin'. I own the place now and rent out the rooms. I keep the gardens goin'. I think I'll stay here forever." She was proud of all she'd done and she had done a lot. I was proud of her too. I told her so.

"Miss Kate, I need help. I got a girl I got to go find but I need a car. Before that, I need a job. Got anything I can do?" I had been right to go to her. Miss Kate had me to work in an hour's time, fencing in her gardens. I guess the deer had been getting in, and she wanted to keep them out.

I worked for Miss Kate for four weeks. After putting in that fence, I repaired most of the rooms in the house. It was a lot of work. All of the rooms were in need of paint. The stairs needed repairs. After I finished all that, Miss Kate wanted me to look at the kitchen. I rehung most of the cabinet doors and straightened the shelving. Inna was always on my mind.

After a month, Miss Kate had a surprise for me. Somewhere, somehow, she had found me a car. It was nothing fancy but it ran—it would get me to Inna. She gave me my pay and kissed me on the cheek. "Now, go get your Inna, Jurak. Love each other enough for all of us."

As I drove away, I looked in my rear-view mirror and saw her wipe her cheek.

I drove most of that night and made it to one of the ugliest, small-town main streets I had ever been through. North Dakota was flat, and this town was set right on it like it had never settled into the land. There were a few trees but they were small, starved looking things. The buildings couldn't have been more than twenty or thirty years old but were so sun-bleached and wind-blown, they looked older. When I pulled in to the only filling station, a man walked out real slow. He asked who I was and where I was going.

I told him I was looking for Inna and asked if he knew where to go from there. He looked me up. Then, he looked me down. I guess I didn't look too bad because he pointed northwards. "Go about five miles; ya can't miss it." Then, he took my money and went back inside.

I glanced up the road and took a deep breath. I was only five miles away from her. All that night, I hadn't doubted a thing, I only thought about her and getting to her. Worry settled in. What was I going to say? I had nothing, only promises and hope.

I pulled the car back onto that main road and headed north. It seemed a much shorter distance than five miles, and, the whole time, my stomach had that weird pinching feeling. The guy who owned that gas station had been correct. I couldn't have missed the farm. It seemed like it was the only house for miles around.

I slowed down and pulled into the yard.

A woman came out the front door. She had to be Inna's mother. She was short, and her nose turned up the same way. Her cheeks and figure were fuller, but there was no mistaking the resemblance. I wondered what her name was and didn't know what to say or how to greet her.

"You must be Jurak?" She didn't smile but she didn't ask me to leave either. I was surprised she knew my name. Some of the pinching feeling left my stomach.

"Yes, ma'am. I am Jurak. I was wondering, is Inna here? I drove over to talk to her today." I had no idea what I was saying, but, God, it sounded dumb. I drove over to talk to her? Today? I lived a good ten hours away; it wasn't just some small thing. I leaned back to look at the house.

It was a tall farmhouse. One time it had been white, with bright yellow trim, but both were now faded. It wasn't in neat repair nor disrepair. It was a decent house, bigger than Mama and Nils. There was no grass and no trees. I really was finding North Dakota less than desirable, and I wondered how Inna could have grown up in such a place in such stark contrast to her.

Nothing matched Inna—it was too mundane. Buildings were faded, trees were sparse, and no bright colors penetrated the bleakness of it all. I saw a movement in an upstairs window. I wondered who it was. Feeling more courageous, I approached the woman with my hand out.

"I am Jurak, like you said. I came here to talk with Inna." The woman didn't take my hand. She just backed away a step or two and shook her head. I wondered if she had understood me; she had such a thick accent, and I remembered Inna had told me her parents were from Germany. I tried German, "Hallo, Ich heisse, Jurak. Kann ich mit Inna sprechen?"

"Ja." She laughed a little. She never took my hand but she yelled into the house. I saw the curtain move again.

"Jurak!" And there she was. Inna came hurrying out, "Mama, this is Jurak. I told you about him." She kissed her mother's cheek and came down to the yard to stand by me. All my courage left and my stomach hurt again. I felt stupid. I hadn't really planned beyond driving up there.

Before I knew it, though, I was down on one knee. I didn't care that her mama was watching. I didn't care who else saw me. I did it without thinking. I was kneeling down in front of her and digging in my pocket for the ring I had bought. I looked up at her then and realized what a mistake I had made.

The ring I had worked so hard for was too plain for the amazing woman who stood before me now. She was so short that I was nearly as tall even on my knee. She was more beautiful than I remembered. Her hair was dark and shiny. Her eyes were the brightest blue. She was dressed in pants made of tough material like the Levi's I wore myself. They hugged her tiny waist. I reached for her hand, and, even though I was shaking inside, my hand was steady. My voice was not.

"Inna, I know how stupid this might seem. I drove here to talk to you and I know, I know, we only met a short while, but it was enough time for me to know you're the one for me. I don't want anyone else." I held onto her hands but I didn't put that ring on her finger just yet. I looked into her eyes. She wasn't smiling.

I let go of her hand. Then, I picked it up again. I dropped the ring. I let go of her hand again and dug around in the dirt till I found it. I polished it on my shirt and tried to get the nerve up to ask what I came here to ask. I looked up at her.

Her eyes were so blue, the sky couldn't even compare. She smiled then. I noticed her right cheek had a slight dimple. I lost my voice. Why on Earth would she want anything to do with me? I dropped the ring again. I felt my shoulders drop as I looked for it once again, but you know what? While I was facing the dirt, I reminded myself I was a Devil. I won the war. *I was living.* I had promised myself that after that damn war, I wasn't going to miss out on life anymore.

I straightened my shoulders, polished that ring again, and grabbed her left hand. "Inna, I know we don't have a plan. We don't really know each other, but I know you're the one for me. I know it. I don't want to miss out on life anymore. Just say yes, Inna. Say yes to being my wife. Please?" Miraculously, she didn't pull away.

She looked down at the ring, plain as it was, and, somehow, her eyes grew brighter. "Yes, Jurak, I will marry you. Yes!" I could hardly believe my ears. For reasons I could never comprehend, Inna said yes.

I couldn't contain myself; I picked her up and twirled her around. I kissed her eyes, her cheeks, and, finally, her lips. I held her close thinking I would never let go.

"Let me get my things, Jurak. I packed the other day and have been waiting for you, just in case." She turned and headed back to the house. Her mama was smiling and wiping tears from her cheeks. Inna gave her a hug and the woman nodded to her daughter. Her mother understood there was nothing for Inna here.

I walked over and hugged her mother and thanked her for understanding. I promised I would look after Inna and take care of her. It seemed a long time before Inna returned. She had that same small suitcase she carried on the bus. She had changed into a neat little blue suit with a matching hat. It matched her eyes perfectly.

I took the case and put it in the back, alongside mine. I settled Inna into the front seat and hurried around to get in myself. She was yelling to her mother, "I love you, Mama! Tell Papa I love him, and we will see you real soon!" It was then I noticed a white fluffy cat, sitting atop a fence post, licking her front paw. Her tail stood straight up and turned at a funny angle; she glanced our way, and I swore I saw her smile.

I got in, started the car, and asked Inna where she wanted to go. "I hear Coeur de' Laine is pretty. Let's go there." Italy quickly turned into a terrible fight for survival each and every day. My training is all that saved me. I fought and even killed without second-guessing myself, without thinking what actions needed to come next. I quickly learned the fighting is just one horror of war. War, is so much more than hunting and killing the enemy. I was shocked to learn that humans can live subjected to such horrible, demeaning circumstances.

Soldiers are displaced with no real place to rest. Each day we faced the elements. We learned to ignore the heat, cold, rain, and snow. Continually being exposed to the elements made our skin calloused and red. Our hair grew longer than standard regulations and we were generally grimy. Ironically, we tried to shave every day. Everyone battled bugs. They crawled through our clothes and hair. We changed and washed our clothes when we were able but honestly, I always thought our numbers were doubled as our uniforms could have stood and fought on their own. We smelled so bad the only thing hiding us from the Nazis was their own stench.

No one had to teach me to hate or fear the mud. I learned quickly enough; mud was a real enemy. Mud made walking impossible. It got into everything and I hated its taste. Mud ruined everything. It held the cold, the wet, and the bugs. Thick mud barred us from any quick successes. Mud was the ever-present and constant threat.

The beauty of Italy did not escape me. If we hadn't been fighting, it was a place I thought I would have liked to visit or even live. It was so different from home. Cobblestone streets and old buildings were everywhere, even on the mountainside. Nothing was wild.

Nineteen forty-three was all war, we fought every single day and as the year deepened, so did our resolve. We were the elite and proud of it. We fought without thinking, killed without caring, and were feared. They called us the Devils in Baggy pants.

One morning, bright and early, we moved through a tiny village that boasted only a few houses and one small church. As we moved through, I noticed movement to my right. Ever at the ready, I raised my rifle. There was no enemy instead I noticed a small child, a girl of about seven years, watching us from the shadows of a small doorway. She had big eyes full of fear. No one else seemed to notice or care to notice her.

We continued on, but that little face haunted me. She was all alone. As I walked through her small village, I saw no other living person. We left her behind even though she was so small and vulnerable. There was nowhere to take her. I reminded myself I was a soldier, responsible for killing. That was the harsh truth. We were only responsible for one duty. There was no time or energy to care for children. I was nothing more than a Devil, bringing hell across a war-weary land.

By the end of December, we had dug in and were waiting for orders. As hard as we fought, the Nazis fought back just as hard. The idea we might take Rome fast and easy were sidelined and forgotten. Rome was not going to fall easily. Both sides wanted the victory and we were nearly stalemated at Anzio.

Anzio was the Nazi's last defense and they were going to keep it at all costs. The fight was horrifying and lasted more than four months. Nothing won that fight but sheer willpower; two American commanders were removed from duty, I thought, unfairly, due our lack of success. Most of us enlisted resigned ourselves to the fate of painful death.

It was terrible. It was laborious gaining any ground. Each move was difficult. We gained ground then dug in. Houses, church towers, and shops all hid our enemy if we weren't already utilizing those spaces. We, the invaders, fought against the unknown.

The streets were a mystery and the language unknown. Such obstacles only aided the enemy securing their knowledge of everything we couldn't know.

It felt more like World War One than Two. Lines were drawn, sides would dig in behind them. Small spaces of land were won and new lines drawn. Over and again. We killed, were killed and finally in May 1944, we took it. That victory was so hard-won, we hardly called it victory. There were so many dead, the 504s so depleted, we were sent to England for short respite.

When I left home I was young, but battle aged me. I wasn't even sure how to take respite. The Brits welcomed us alright. We drank, smoke, grabbed any girl we could and did our best to live up to our Devilish reputation. A week into respite, I didn't feel anymore rested than the first day.

I looked around. I was surrounded by empty stuck open eyes focusing on distant spaces. Pretty girls walked around smiling at us, but I barely registered them. I grabbed one and kissed her, full on the mouth, ready to somehow end my suffering with her love. Her arms around my neck, her mouth open, I found myself clinging to her, trying to be human again. I was crying into her hair, and so afraid of letting go. She let me hold on and then stepped away, I hadn't asked her name and I didn't even watch her go. I grabbed another bottle and drank as deep as I could, praying for a release from my sins. Music played on through the night and more girls came through. Not one of us followed anyone out that night. We sat, in a row, our eyes stuck open, staring into the nothingness that had become life.

Over the next few days, I slowly began to feel human again. I stared less but I hated loud noises. Every time someone laughed too loud or shouted, I jumped. I couldn't figure it out. I was never jumpy on the battlefield. I couldn't make sense of why I was so jumpy while I was safe and quiet in England. There were no children in harm's way and I wasn't protecting my comrades but this was somehow worse. I relentlessly thought of so many others who were in danger. I constantly felt guilty for my hard-earned respite. Every night I desperately tried to live.

God, I wanted to live. I wanted to drink every drop of life offered to me. I wanted to taste food, sleep until I was rested, feel every woman and watch the sun come up every morning. I didn't want to miss out on anything. I was a soldier, though, in an unstoppable war.

We were asked to volunteer for more. We weren't told but we all guessed, the Allies were finally ready to invade France. I wanted no part.

The moment they began telling us what was needed, that horrible pinching feeling in my stomach returned with such a force, I nearly passed out. Me, a battle-hearted Devil wearing baggy pants, nearly fell over. When they asked, I didn't raise my hand. We were all told it was fine, our unit was one of the hardest hit in Italy and that was why we were being given a choice. In the end, only three guys volunteered. Guilt, that would last a lifetime, washed over me as I walked away.

I had seen too much, fought too hard and just killed too many to join. I wanted to live. After these few days off, I wanted it more than anything. I went outside to calm myself and smoke. I found a patch of mostly dry ground, something of a commodity in England, and stood smoking and thinking. I could feel my eyes open, staring past everything.

Breathing deeply, I stood, waiting to come back. The smoke curled around my face and after a few minutes, I noticed a cat was sitting at my feet.

She was white, fluffy and her tail bent at a strange angle. She looked up at me, with piercing blue eyes and reached her paw onto my boot. I blinked and she was gone.